SPELLBOUND
A HARENGON & DRAGONBORN TALE

NESTA WILLARD

Spellbound: A Harengon & Dragonborn Tale

"Three souls. One destiny. In the battle between light and darkness, who will rise and who will fall?"

Nesta Willard

copyright

Title: *Spellbound*
Subtitle: *A Harengon and Dragonborn Tale*
Author: Nesta Willard

© 2025 Nesta Willard
All rights reserved.
No part of this book may be reproduced, stored, or distributed in any form or by any means, electronic or mechanical, including photocopying or recording, without the prior written permission of the author, except for brief quotations used in reviews or critical articles.

This is a work of fiction. Names, characters, places, and events are products of the author's imagination or used fictitiously. Any resemblance to actual events, locales, or persons living or dead is purely coincidental.

Contains mature themes, violence, and explicit content intended for adult audiences.

ISBN: 978-1-326-42428-2

Cover Design by Nesta Willard
Interior Design by Nesta Willard

Table of Contents

1. Dedication
2. Acknowledges
3. To the readers
4. The Encounter
5. The Cost of Control
6. Hopps's Past
7. The Breaking Point
8. Astryd's Past
9. Breaking the Walls
10. The Quiet Push
11. Astryd's Decision
12. The Long Road Ahead
13. The Road Less Travelled
14. Underneath the Moonlit Veil
15. Into the Dark
16. Blood and Bone
17. Into the Abyss
18. The Heart of the Forest
19. Shadows in the Stone
20. The Edge of the Abyss
21. The Whispering Ruins
22. The Weight of the Relic
23. Clash of Shadows
24. Unravelling Threads
25. The Edge of Desperation

26. The Depths of Darkness
27. Fury Unbound
28. The Breaking of the Circle
29. The Price of Power
30. Fractures and Flame
31. The Tethered Path
32. The Gathering Storm
33. The Final Stand
34. Surrounded by Shadows
35. The Last Veil
36. The Heart's Command
37. Through Smoke and Silence
38. The Shattered Sigil
39. The Relic's Choice
40. A Bond Forged in Flame
41. Ashes and Oaths
42. The Circle Reclaimed
43. The Burden We Carry
44. Rise Through Ruin
45. A Reckoning of Blood
46. No Gods Above
47. The Path We Choose
48. Scars Beneath the Skin
49. The Storm's Edge
50. The Fire We Wield
51. Through the Ashes

52. The Price of Belief
53. First Strike
54. The Tides of War
55. The Bonds We Defend
56. Through Fire and Fear
57. The Line Between
58. Blades and Blood
59. The Victory
60. What Remains
61. The Last Light
62. Sanctuary Bound
63. The Final Thread
64. Coming Soon: Sanctum of Flame
65. Bonus chapter Chapter One: Where Peace Starts to Crack
66. Authors note
67. Acknowledgment
68. To the readers
69. Thank you

Dedication

To Sofie
You're my chaos twin. My co-creator.
The voice behind Hopps, and the reason this story exists.
What started as a joke a bard who wouldn't shut up,
and a sorcerer who wanted to set him on fire
became something deeper. Truer. Unstoppable.

You made Hopps unforgettable. I gave Astryd her fury. Together, we let them fall. This story is our wild, tender, and full of heart.
Forged in late-night chaos, shared laughter,
And D&D tension that turned into something real.

Here's to the one bed. The stolen glances.
The slow surrender. To every night in the tent just me and Hopps.

Thank you for the fire, the magic, and the story. We built this world together.
Let it burn beautifully.

To Toni
For Blu, who brought the light when all seemed lost,
A guiding hand through the storm, no matter the cost.
In every shadow, in every fight, She rose like dawn, chasing the night.

Her strength a flame that never wavered. Her heart a beacon, fiercely savoured.

In the darkest corners, where hope was thin,
You made her the spark that made them win.
With every battle, with every breath, You helped her overcome fear, defy death.

Blu became the light they all needed, Her courage a shield, her will undefeated.

Thank you for the light, for the strength you gave, For guiding Blu through every wave. In this world we crafted, bound in the dark, You helped her shine an unyielding spark.

Acknowledgments

To our players. Our party.
To every chaotic D&D session that somehow turned horny
Thank you.

Thank you for the unhinged ideas that absolutely should've gotten us
killed,
    The laughter so loud it broke concentration checks,
and the dice rolls that defied physics, logic, and morality but still led us straight into glory.

You brought the chaos. You brought the charm. And you sure as hell brought the heat.

This story is stitched together from nat 1s, innuendo, and questionable decisions
Held together by flirt-fuelled spells and nights in the tent
where it was just me and Hopps… and no one dared cast *Zone of Truth.*

You didn't just keep the fire burning. You fed it whiskey, dared it to get hotter, and then rolled for initiative when it did.

You made disaster look like destiny. Turned every failed plan into a plot twist.
And somehow made horny bards the backbone of emotional storytelling.

Thank you for the madness. For the magic. For making this world a place where horny bards thrive,
sorcerers blush, and no camping trip is ever safe again.

Here's to the one-bed trope. To natural 20s in all the wrong places.
To eye contact across the fire and spells that feel like confessions.
To saying "I cast Fireball" when you really mean "I love you."
To never playing it safe, on or off the battlefield.

Here's to bad decisions, full-send rolls, and never sleeping alone in the tent.

We didn't just play with fire.
We became it.

To the Readers

This isn't a story of love at first sight.
It's a story of tension slow, sharp, and impossible to ignore.
Of obsession sparked the moment power met resistance.
Of a bard who speaks in smirks, in silence, in secrets.
And a sorceress who trusts no one but herself.

She wanted control. Solitude. But he made her feel.
With fury. With fire. With him.

She never meant to understand him. He never meant to want her surrender. But the relic bound them, exposed them And now, neither can walk away.

A sorceress who commands the battlefield. A bard who sees through every wall she builds. And a bond forged in the fires of conflict,
One no force can easily break.

But they are not alone anymore.

A Dragonborn cleric. A fierce protector. A sanctuary in skin.
She joins their fight not to follow, but to anchor.
Not to soften the story, but to sharpen its truth.
A trio forged in power, in pain, in earned trust.
One that doesn't just survive the fire it wields it.

This story isn't soft. It's not tame.
It doesn't ask permission. It challenges. It claws.
It carves space for love that looks like war,
And healing that doesn't whisper it roars.

And if you're still here, still reading,
Then maybe you're ready too.

Ready for the weight of a relic pressed to your chest.
Ready for choice, for challenge, for change.
For fire in all its forms rage, passion, rebirth.

So read on. Lean in. Let it burn.
But don't expect to walk away unchanged.

Nesta Willard

Chapter One: The Encounter

The world had never been quiet. Not really.

Even without sound, Hopps could feel the pulse of it the way tavern floorboards vibrated beneath heavy boots, the flicker of candle flames shifting with breath and movement, the crackle of tension rolling off people like smoke from a fire they were trying too hard to hide.

He didn't need ears to hear any of that.

And tonight? The whole room was humming.

Because she was here.

Astryd.

He'd only learned her name two towns ago, spelled out in sharp, irritated signs after she finally snapped and told him to leave her alone.

Gods, it had been beautiful.

She was beautiful. Even when she hated him. Especially when she hated him.

She hadn't noticed him yet or she was pretending not to. Either way, Hopps watched her from the corner of the tavern, half-hidden in shadow. Her cloak was dark, her hood up, her presence like a spell she didn't need to cast dangerous, elegant, untouchable. She was a flicker of flame at the edge of a battlefield, and he couldn't stop staring.

She was reading again, lips parted in concentration over some ancient scroll, like the fate of the realm was hidden in dusty lines of magic only she could understand. She hadn't looked at him once. Didn't matter.

Hopps raised a hand and signed across the tavern, lazy and slow, just to irritate her: *"**Miss me?**"*

No response. Just a flick of her fingers beneath the table. A flash.

A dagger illusory but realistic as sin whipped through the air and sank into the wall beside his head. The patrons around him jumped.

Hopps grinned, unbothered.

Gods, she was fun.

He made a mental note to compliment her illusion work. Later. After she threatened his life again. Probably with fire this time.

Drink in hand, he moved through the crowd. Quiet. Confident. People always underestimated how silent a bard could be when he wasn't speaking. When he was just… watching.

And watching her? That was the only thing that mattered.

She didn't flinch when he sat across from her. Didn't look up. Didn't acknowledge him at all. The tavern roared around them, but between them? Silence. Electric.

He waited.

And when she gave him nothing, he lifted his hands and signed: *"You know, stalking's only a crime if it's not mutual."*

Finally, she looked up. Not at his hands at him.

Her eyes were fire and steel. No softness. No tolerance. No mercy. Only warning.

Perfect.

Hopps smiled a slow, predatory thing and leaned back, stretching like he owned the space. He liked her like this. Liked how she tried to make him small with her gaze, how she thought she could intimidate him with just a look.

He signed again, more deliberate this time: *"You know you want me. You're just waiting for me to make the first move."*

Astryd didn't break her gaze. Her fingers twitched barely a flick, too fast for anyone to notice but him.

Another illusion dagger cut through the air, stopping just short of his throat. Hovering. Humming with power.

He didn't flinch. Didn't blink.

"Harder next time," he mouthed.

A flicker of something broke through her façade a crack in the mask. Just the smallest twitch at the corner of her mouth.

He'd seen it. He wanted to see more.

Hopps leaned forward, just close enough to catch her scent magic, leather, the warmth of a woman too powerful to be contained. His fingers brushed the edge of her scroll, light as a caress.

He signed: ***"Still pretending you don't like it when I watch?"***

No response. Not that he expected one.

Her fingers moved again beneath the table.

Another illusion dagger. This one landed in the wood beside his ear, the magic so potent he could feel it reverberate in his chest.

A warning. A challenge.

Hopps sat back and smiled wider.

"You're getting better at this," he signed.

She rolled her eyes. A sigh, barely perceptible. He wasn't going anywhere, and she knew it.

"You're insufferable," she said under her breath.

He leaned in with a flash of teeth. ***"But charming."***

"Like a rash." she says

He smirked. ***"Rashes go away."***

"You're assuming I won't make you disappear."

"I'm betting you won't," he said, and then grinned. ***"Because you'd miss me."***

She glared. ***"You've been following me for three towns."***

"And yet you keep letting me catch up. Curious."

Another illusion blade sparked to life this one hovering directly over his groin.

Hopps raised both hands in mock surrender.

"Alright, alright. I'll behave."

"You don't know how."

He signed: *"No. But I can learn."*

She stared at him for a long time, then muttered, *"Doubtful."*

Still, the blade vanished.

Hopps tilted his head. *"So... dinner?"*

She stood without a word. Her cloak flared behind her like wings.

"Where are you going?" he signed quickly.

"Anywhere you're not," she said, striding toward the door.

He followed.

"Walk faster," she snapped without turning around.

"Make me."

She stopped. Turned. Stepped into his space so fast it made him blink.

"I don't play games."

Hopps swallowed. *"I do."* he signed

"Then play alone."

He stepped even closer, their boots nearly touching. *"You keep saying that,"* he signed, *"but you haven't left me bleeding yet."*

Her brow arched. *"Don't tempt me."*

"Oh, I live to tempt you."

She summoned another dagger this one slower, deliberate. It hovered between them, shimmering like liquid fire.

He held her gaze. Stepped into it.

The illusion passed clean through his chest, harmless, but the heat of her magic was real. It prickled along his skin like static, like a warning.

"Try again," he signed.

She shoved him. Not hard but enough.

He stumbled back a step, laughing. ***"There she is."***

"Last warning," she said.

He signed with a grin*:* ***"You walk first."***

A flicker of genuine surprise crossed her face.

Then, slowly, she signed it back: ***"You walk first."***

Hopps's breath hitched. But he didn't mock her. He knew what that meant.

It wasn't a dismissal.

It was a line. A boundary. A promise not yet broken.

He didn't move.

Not yet.

The moment hung between them thick, breathless, electric.

For a long moment, they stared at each other. No blinking. No backing down.

She didn't say it aloud this time. She didn't need to.

Her fingers moved once more measured, certain.

Hopps watched the sharp lines of her sign, the weight of each word landing like a blow: ***"You walk first."***

It wasn't the first time she'd said it. But this time, it felt different.

Like she meant it.

Like she trusted him to listen.

It wasn't a rejection. It wasn't an end.

It was a challenge. A boundary. A line not yet meant to be crossed.

For the first time in a long while, Hopps was forced to wait.

But he wasn't afraid.

He wasn't frustrated.

He was... patient. Ready.

Because he knew that one day, when the time was right, something would shift.

And when it did, they'd both know.

In that moment, all he could do was watch her silent, waiting. But not to break her. Not to win her.

To understand her.

And maybe, eventually, to stand beside her.

Then finally, with a breath held and a nod exchanged, Hopps rose. He turned, slow and certain, and walked away.

But not far.

Never far.

Chapter Two: The Cost of Control

She didn't want him.
Not as company.
Not as backup.
Not even as a distraction.

Hopps was the kind of Harengon who thrived on chaos. He chased fire like it was a game and she was fire. Unforgiving. Untouchable. A blaze that no one should dare to get close to.

He didn't belong in her orbit.

And yet… he followed.

Not like prey.
Like gravity.
Irresistible. Relentless.

She felt him before she saw him. His presence was a subtle pressure in the air, something she couldn't ignore. Like a storm building behind her back. The way he moved quiet, sure was infuriating. As if he were claiming space she never gave him permission to enter.

His eyes tracked her every movement, a heat behind them that she could feel more than see. She didn't have to look to know. It was like his focus wrapped around her spine and squeezed.

She hated him for it.

She hated the way he stood there, unspoken and still, saying everything with nothing at all. She hated the way her pulse quickened when she caught his scent on the wind pine and mischief and something old she couldn't name.

She hated the way he made her feel seen. Exposed.

But mostly, she hated the way part of her wanted him to keep looking.

Astryd gritted her teeth and pressed forward. The alley was dim and narrow, carved between old stone buildings with moss lining their base. A shortcut she didn't need but took anyway, as if distance would somehow dissolve the pull in her chest.

He followed. Of course he did.

And this time, there was no hiding from it.

The click of her boots echoed in rhythm with her pulse. She didn't allow herself to look over her shoulder. Not once. But the tension inside her built with every step. Every breath dragged the scent of tavern smoke and cold night air through her nose and underneath it, him.

She tried to push it down. To keep her walls high. But something about him was different.

He thinks he can get to me. He's wrong.

Her hands clenched into fists. Magic flared beneath her skin cold, sharp, insistent. A living current that coiled through her veins. She welcomed the pain of it. Let it burn through the edges of her restraint.

She was Warlock-born.
Sorcerer-forged.
Untouchable.

And yet, despite all of that… the air had shifted. Thicker now. The night pressed against her skin, and beneath it, the quiet weight of him. Present. Intentional.

She turned sharply into another alley. Her heartbeat was a war drum behind her ribs. She didn't slow. Didn't let herself.

The buildings rose tighter around her, casting shadows that swallowed her in silence. Her breath came sharper now, clouding in the cold, her fists still clenched at her sides. She told herself it was the magic. That it was just adrenaline. Just anger.

But it wasn't.

It was him.

Hopps wasn't following her any more.

He was haunting her steps.

The difference was subtle. But she felt it. He wasn't chasing. He wasn't provoking. He wasn't trying to get under her skin. He was simply… there. Existing in her space. Holding it without permission and without apology.

And it was working. She hated that.

Her pace faltered as she reached the end of the alley. The sounds of the city had faded behind them left in tavern warmth and candlelight. Here, it was stone and breath and shadow.

And him.

She didn't turn right away. But she knew. He was behind her. A step or two back. Waiting.

She could feel his silence pressing between her shoulder blades like a hand.

She closed her eyes. Took a slow breath. Let her magic rise through her throat like a scream she wouldn't let out. Just enough to warn. To threaten.

Then she turned.

Hopps stood in the alley mouth, arms crossed, one ear twitching slightly in the night breeze. That damned smirk again. The one that wasn't mocking. Just… knowing.

His eyes locked on hers, calm and quiet and endless.

Astryd stepped forward. Her posture straight. Shoulders squared. *"I don't want you here,"* she said. The words came sharp. Cold. Like the blade she wished she could throw between them.

He didn't move.

She stepped closer. Close enough to see the twitch of muscle in his jaw. The barely-contained energy in his stillness.

She wanted him to flinch. To retreat.

He didn't.

The air between them pulsed.

"I said," she growled, *"I don't want you here."*

Still, he remained silent. But his silence was louder than any shout. It echoed.

"You think I'm something to be won?" she demanded.

He shook his head slowly. One motion. Simple. Certain.

Her jaw clenched. She wanted to scream. To summon fire. To make him bleed just to feel something move. Her magic surged again, hot this time, wild in her chest like a second heartbeat.

It shimmered along her arms faint lines of light crawling like cracks in porcelain.

Hopps saw it.

And still, he didn't move.

She hated him for that, too.

She took one more step. Close enough now that his scent hit her fully pine, heat, old magic and something she didn't recognize. Something she wanted to.

"You're not going anywhere, are you?" she asked. Quieter now. A whisper pulled from the edge of exhaustion.

Hopps didn't respond.

He just… stayed. And that more than anything unravelled her. Her hands fell to her sides. The magic faded. Not gone. Just… quieter.

She was tired. Of running. Of fighting. Of pretending he wasn't there when she could feel every breath between them.

She looked at him really looked. And for the first time, she didn't see a nuisance or a pest. She saw someone who hadn't turned away.   Not once.
          Not even when she'd wanted him to. And that scared her more than anything. She wasn't running any more. She wasn't fighting him. She was just… waiting.

Waiting for whatever came next.

Chapter Three: Hopps's Past

Hopps was used to being alone.
Not just comfortable with it he had built himself out of it.

Solitude wasn't a curse. It was structure. It was safety.
It was the one thing that never betrayed him.

People? They were unpredictable. Messy. They asked for things they had no right to. Made promises they never intended to keep.

So Hopps learned. Learned that silence couldn't lie to him. That empty space was better than empty words.

He wore loneliness like armor and silence like a blade. But it hadn't always been that way.

There was a time he'd lived wide open. A time when joy came easy, and trust was as natural as breathing. His world had been laughter and motion and music life moving too fast to question.

He used to sing with his whole chest. He used to tell stories like they mattered. He used to believe in people. And then she happened. The one who taught him how deep betrayal could cut.

She'd been everything his partner in quests, his sparring match in words, his fire at his back. He didn't fall in love with her like in the songs. He ran into love with her, headlong and reckless, the way only fools and poets do.

And she'd let him. She let him believe. Until the night she didn't.

No goodbye.
No warning.
Just gone.

One moment, she was at his side, fingers brushing his as they read the last line of a prophecy that could change everything. And the next? Smoke. Ash. Silence.

And a relic gone missing.

And gods… Hopps had been so sure.

So fucking sure that she believed in him too.

But she didn't. She never had. And the worst part?

She took more than trust with her.

She took his voice.

Because when he tried to speak after that tried to explain what happened, tried to make sense of the way she disappeared no one listened.

Worse they pitied him.
Treated him like a fool.
Like a man left behind by a woman who never planned to stay.

He hated that.

So he stopped speaking. Not because he couldn't, but because he wouldn't.

Words had betrayed him just as much as she had.
He didn't owe the world anything else.

And silence… silence never asked him to be more than what he was.
It let him breathe.

It kept him from breaking.

He became a whisper where he'd once been a song.
A shadow where he'd once been the flame.
But at least he was his own.

That was the day he stopped chasing.

No more partners.
No more promises.
No more soft openings in the shape of trust.

Just the road, the silence, and the ache in his chest he didn't talk about.

Until her.

Astryd.

He didn't know what to make of her. Not really.
She wasn't like the one who left no, Astryd was something *else* entirely.

She didn't make promises. She didn't lie pretty.
She stood tall, teeth bared, power coiled under her skin like lightning.

She didn't run from fire **she was fire**.

But it wasn't just her strength that caught him. It was the fracture beneath it.
The way she held herself together with tension so tight it could slice open gods.

She reminded him of a blade sharpened too many times dangerous not just to enemies, but to herself.

And he saw it.

The way she pushed people back. The way she never looked too long, never let her voice crack. She fought vulnerability like it was a war she'd already lost once.

He knew that war.

He wore the same scars.

And maybe that was why he couldn't walk away.

Not this time.

Not from someone who reminded him what it felt like to be known and still afraid.

Because deep down, buried beneath layers of magic and mistrust, Astryd wasn't just powerful.

She was *wounded*.
She was *lonely*.
She was *furious*.

And Hopps?
He didn't want to tame her.

Didn't want to fix her.
Didn't want to touch her scars and call it love.

He just wanted to *stay*.

To be something constant in a world that had only ever taken from them both.
Not to earn her affection. Not to prove himself worthy.
Just to stand there. Quiet. Present. Unmoving.

A force as patient as she was fierce.

She didn't know it yet.
Maybe she never would.

But he would wait.

Not because he needed her.
Because he saw her.

And maybe… just maybe… one day, she'd see him too.

And she'd understand the truth no one had ever told them:

You don't always need to be saved.
Sometimes, you just need someone who refuses to leave.

Chapter Four: The Breaking Point

Astryd

She hadn't meant to come back.

She'd told herself she was done. That she was walking away. That she was in control. But her feet had carried her here anyway. Back into the stillness. Back into the heat she couldn't shake. Back into the tavern into the place where he always managed to find her.

"No. Absolutely not."

The words came out as soon as he stepped into view, and Astryd didn't even flinch when she saw Hopps standing in the doorway of the old tavern, that infuriating smirk already spreading across his face.

"You're not coming with me."

Her voice was sharp, cutting through the air, every word laced with as much force as she could muster. She took a step forward, her body language making it clear that this was not a request. She was done playing his games. Done letting him slip under her skin, inch by inch.

The tavern was empty except for them. Dust clung to every surface, and the low light gave the space a warped, dreamlike edge. Shadows shifted in the corners. A broken chandelier creaked overhead, swaying slightly as if stirred by the force of her fury alone.

Hopps didn't say a word. His silence was more oppressive than any speech, and it made her blood boil. He didn't need to speak. He just stood there, his calmness the very thing that rubbed her raw.

Astryd clenched her fists. *"I don't need you. I don't want you,"* she spat, the words thick with the fire of frustration building in her chest. *"Stay out of my way."*

Hopps raised an eyebrow, still silent. That damnable, knowing look in his eyes only made her more furious.

You don't get to decide that, he seemed to say with just the tilt of his head. His hands stayed at his sides relaxed, but full of quiet strength. He didn't have to speak. She knew the words he wasn't saying.

Astryd was not in the mood for this game. She didn't care how much he thought he knew her. He didn't know anything. She wasn't going to let him worm his way into her life, into her quest, into her.

"I'm not asking for your help," she bit out, stepping even closer, feeling the heat of her anger rise. *"I didn't need it then, and I don't need it now. I'm doing this alone. I don't need you breathing down my neck."*

Hopps didn't flinch. He didn't blink. His eyes never left hers, as though he were watching her unravel and was content to let her rage. That only made her more furious.

"You don't belong here!" she shouted, throwing her hands out in frustration. "I didn't ask for you to follow me. *I didn't ask for any of this. You, you are nothing but a distraction! I don't need someone like you around getting in my way, testing my patience!"*

Her voice cracked slightly, but she didn't let it stop her. She wasn't going to show weakness. She couldn't.

Astryd spun on her heel, pacing in a tight circle, trying to force her mind to stay focused, to keep pushing, but her thoughts were spinning. Every time she looked at him, she was reminded of the draw the pull in her gut that told her he was getting closer to something she didn't want him to reach.

She couldn't let him in. She wouldn't.

Her boots scraped sharply across the warped floor as she turned again, magic simmering beneath her skin, restless and sharp. The air around her felt electric too charged, too full and he was the storm cloud at the centre of it.

"What do you think you're going to do, huh?" she snapped, spinning to face him again. *"Get close? Get into my head? Break me down with your silence, your presence?"* She laughed, the sound bitter and unsteady. *"You're not getting under my skin, Hopps. You're not. Do you hear me?"*

Hopps remained unmoved. He stepped forward just enough that she could feel the air between them shift, but still, he didn't speak.

"Stop looking at me," she hissed, voice seething. *"Stop watching me. Stop trying to be what I don't need. Stop."*

She felt heat behind her eyes, and her voice thinned dangerously. A storm of emotion swelled in her chest rage, confusion, panic. It clawed at her ribcage like it wanted out, like it wanted to burn everything down, including him.

Her breath caught, frustration building until she couldn't hold it in any more. She slammed her hands down on the table beside her. The wood buckled beneath the force, and a crack splintered across its surface as her magic flared uncontrolled.

"You don't get to play with me like this. I won't let you!"

But Hopps wasn't playing with her. He wasn't playing at all. He wasn't here for games. He was here for something else something he didn't have to vocalize. And that was infuriating.

Astryd turned away, biting her lip so hard she tasted copper. She was losing control, and she hated it. She had fought too hard to get here, too hard to carve out her own path, to be alone only to have this Harengon show up and exist in her space. His presence was like a weight that pressed down on her, a silent pressure she couldn't throw off.

"Why are you doing this?" she asked, her voice quieter now, the anger turning into something deeper, darker. *"Why can't you just leave me alone? I don't need you. I don't want you here. What is it that you want from me?"*

Finally, Hopps stepped closer, closing the distance between them. And despite every fiber of her being screaming at her to step back, she stood firm.

He didn't speak. He didn't have to. But there was a shift in the air something she could feel in her bones. It wasn't physical, but it was there. An unspoken understanding that made her heart race.

She glared at him, waiting for him to break the silence, but he didn't. His gaze softened for just a moment. He didn't look angry. He didn't look smug.

He just looked… present.

And that… that was worse.

Astryd felt her walls begin to crack. Her whole body was tense, trembling slightly with the effort of holding it all in. Not just the magic. Not just the rage. But the fear. The ache. The buried part of her that didn't know what it would do if someone like him stayed.

"No," she breathed, shaking her head, as if the mere thought of him having this much of an effect on her would undo something inside her. "*I don't need you,*" she repeated, more to herself than to him.

Hopps took another step slow, deliberate. But there was no aggression in his movements. He wasn't pushing. He wasn't demanding.

He was offering.

"I'm not asking for you to need me," his silence seemed to say. *"I'm asking if you can accept that you're not alone."*

The realization hit her like a punch to the gut.

She had been fighting him all this time, but something about his quiet resolve was cutting through her defenses in a way nothing else had.

She could feel the tension rising in her chest a tight, unbearable pressure, like something shifting inside her. Something she didn't want to name.

She hated the part of her that didn't want him to go.

"Stop looking at me like that," she demanded, her voice breaking.

Hopps didn't say anything.

He didn't need to.

He wasn't leaving. He wasn't backing down.

And for the first time, Astryd realized something she hadn't let herself face until now.

She wasn't fighting him any more.
She was waiting.
Waiting for him to move.
Waiting for something to give.
Waiting for herself to stop pretending she didn't care.

Chapter Five: Astryd's Past

Astryd

Astryd had always been alone.

Even in a crowd, even surrounded by voices, laughter, or the hum of tavern life she was still apart. The noise never reached her. Not really. There was always a barrier, some invisible wall she had learned to build and reinforce over time.

Even with the magic that coursed through her veins, she remained untouched by the warmth of connection. If anything, the power only made the distance worse. Because no one ever really saw her. They saw the flame. The danger. The warlock-born, sorcerer-forged force of destruction. Not the girl beneath the fire.

She had always carried that weight: alone.

She learned young that the world couldn't be trusted. Trust was a story people told themselves before betrayal. People could be used, discarded, manipulated. They were tools at best, threats at worst. Attachments were liabilities. So she stopped forming them.

She didn't need anyone. She couldn't afford to.

Her powers weren't some blessing. They were a brand. A mark of the bargain she had made the one that had saved her life and stolen it in the same breath. A reminder of the chain wrapped around her soul.

Warlock-blooded. Sorcerer-forged. She hadn't just studied magic she had been carved by it. Transformed. Owned.

She was no stranger to power. She knew how to wield it, how to turn it loose, how to burn down whatever stood in her way. But that power hadn't come freely. It never did.

She had sold her soul for it. Maybe not in the traditional sense, but in ways that mattered more. In choices that could never be taken back. She had traded her freedom, her peace, her ability to breathe without a whisper curling down her spine.

The whispers never stopped.

Her patron didn't thunder commands. They didn't need to. They whispered in the silence. In the breath between heartbeats. When she was falling asleep. When she was bleeding. When she was doubting herself the most.

And she listened. She always listened.

Because they had given her what no one else would power. Purpose. A chance to take control of her life. A chance to become something more than a terrified girl grasping at air while the world tried to crush her.

But that choice… it had come with a price she hadn't understood until it was too late. It wasn't just a magical contract. It wasn't a fair deal.

It was a trap with gilded teeth.

She hadn't given up a piece of herself. She had given up everything.

And the worst part the part that sank its teeth into her late at night when everything was still was that she had wanted it. She had begged for it. She had opened the door and invited the darkness in, believing she could control it.

Now, she wasn't sure there was anything left of her that hadn't been touched by that deal.

Because with that power came the bond. The chain. The constant, gnawing tether she could never sever. It didn't matter how far she ran. It didn't matter how strong she became. The chain was still there. Invisible to others, but she felt it with every spell, every breath.

Her patron didn't force obedience. They didn't need to.

They waited.

Waited for her to stumble. Waited for her to reach for power. Waited for her to need them again.

And she always did.

Every time she pushed the magic too far. Every time she needed to survive. Every time she needed to win.

And every time, they were there smiling in the silence of her mind.

She wanted to rise. Above the pain. Above the weakness that had clung to her like a second skin. Above the desperation and the hunger for something better.

She had told herself she was shaping her own destiny.

But now, she was beginning to see that the very magic she used to lift herself up… was the thing slowly pulling her apart.

Her patron didn't need to bark orders. Their whispers were enough. Their presence had been with her so long it was like a second heartbeat.

A second spine.

A second will, always brushing up against her own.

Every time she channelled power, she felt the tug. The heat. The weight. A reminder that she wasn't just casting spells she was paying for them. With time. With control. With herself.

Her magic was a gift.

But it was also a beautiful, terrifying curse.

And the more she used it, the less she knew where it ended and she began.

It hadn't always been like that. Once, the whispers were faint. The influence was subtle. But now? It was loud. Constant. A presence that gnawed at her thoughts, that curled around her spine and tightened with every passing year.

It had carved space inside her, hollowing out parts she didn't know she'd lost until it was too late.

And that was the truth that chilled her more than anything else.

It would never be enough.

She could never take enough. Never be strong enough. Never be safe enough to stop reaching for more.

And the more she took, the more she lost herself.

Astryd had always been proud of her independence. She clung to it like armor. She wore it like proof that she wasn't weak. That she hadn't been broken.

But she hadn't truly been alone.

Not ever.

The patron was always there. Watching. Whispering. Guiding.

And that meant that no matter how high she rose, no matter how hard she fought she was never really free.

She never would be.

That was the past she never spoke of. The truth she never told.

Especially not to someone like Hopps.

Hopps who didn't know what it felt like to be bound from the inside. Who didn't know what it meant to fight your own thoughts. To be afraid of your own power. To know that the more you fought to reclaim yourself, the more you risked slipping deeper into someone else's grasp.

He didn't know the ache of that silence. The hunger. The *need* to stay in control at all costs.

He didn't know what it felt like to be a weapon one day and a prisoner the next.

And yet there he was.

Still here.

Hopps, with his quiet eyes and maddening calm. With his silence that spoke more than words ever could.

She had told him to leave a dozen times.

And he hadn't.

He didn't press. He didn't demand.

He just stayed.

And it was driving her mad.

Because she had spent *years* turning herself into something untouchable. Something cold. Something even her patron couldn't break.

But Hopps? He didn't try to break her. He just... remained.

And it made her feel things she hadn't let herself feel in years.

Things that were dangerous. Things like wanting. Her magic was a price she paid every day. The cost of survival. The cost of victory. And the longer she fought alone, the more it consumed her.

Because there would always be more to give. More to take. More to lose. The patron had given her everything. And taken everything back. And she had let them. She had let them shape her. Use her. Mold her into something sharp and obedient and strong enough to survive.

And the most painful truth of all? She had no one to blame but herself. That's why she didn't trust. Not with what she carried. Not with what she had become. Not even Hopps. Her past was her own. Her burden. Her chain. No one else's.

But Hopps... He kept showing up. Without promises. Without pressure. Without pretending to understand. He stayed. And something inside her something old and fragile and terrified wanted to reach out.

And that scared her more than anything she had ever faced. Because she didn't need him. She *couldn't* need him**.** ***"I don't need anyone,"*** she whispered, as if saying it aloud might make it true.

But even as the words left her lips, they felt hollow.

Because deep down, in the part of her heart she had locked away for years, she already knew. She wasn't alone any more.

And that truth
That terrifying, unravelling truth
Was more dangerous than any pact she'd ever made.

Chapter Six: Breaking the Walls

Astryd

Astryd had been walking for hours.

The cold bit into her skin, sharp and biting, but she welcomed it. At least the chill was real. Tangible. Unlike the chaos churning inside her chest. Every step forward was meant to shake him off to outpace the feelings she didn't want to name, the questions she refused to ask.

She didn't know how long she'd been walking. Didn't care.

The night air was thin and sharp, filled with the whisper of wind threading through the branches above her. Twigs cracked underfoot, but even the sounds of the forest felt distant muted, like they were happening in another world. The storm inside her drowned out everything else.

Every step took her farther from the tavern and closer to the one place she'd vowed never to go: the edge of herself. The place where she might have to admit she wasn't as strong as she pretended to be.

Where she might have to admit she couldn't do this alone.

The thought made her stomach turn.

She wasn't weak. She had built her life on the refusal to depend on anyone. She didn't ask for help. She didn't *need* help. Not then. Not now.

But Hopps…

Hopps was different. No matter how far she walked. No matter how many times she told him to go. He stayed.

He didn't press. Didn't beg. Didn't try to force her hand.

He simply existed constant and calm, a shadow that never left her side. And the more she resisted him, the more present he seemed to become. Like a tether she never consented to, one she could feel even when he wasn't in sight.

His presence wasn't loud.
It didn't shout or demand.

But it wrapped around her like invisible thread tightening every time she tried to pull away.

"No," she muttered under her breath, as if the word could unbind her.
A denial. A mantra. A shield.

It didn't work.

She wasn't ready for him.
She wasn't ready for what his presence made her feel.

Her heart thundered beneath her ribs, the rhythm too fast, too loud. The tension in her chest had become unbearable. She had survived by building walls higher than anyone could climb. She had weaponized her solitude. People were messy. People broke things broke her.

Magic had been the only thing that never let her down.

It consumed her, yes. But it was always there.
Predictable. Powerful. Hers. She didn't need anyone else. She couldn't.

And yet... She could feel him. Even now. Even here.

Every step she took felt like she was walking in circles closer to him, no matter how hard she tried to run away. Her breath grew ragged, her limbs tense, the ache of resistance settling into her bones.

She pushed herself harder, faster, trying to outrun it.
Outrun *him*.

But he wasn't chasing. He didn't need to. He was waiting. And somehow, that was worse.

Every time she thought she had escaped every time she thought she had won he was there. Just outside her reach. Just inside her skin. Watching. Patient. Present.

She hated him for it. Because it was working.

Without realizing it, she stopped.

Her body refused to take another step. The silence around her pressed in like a heavy cloak. The trees watched. The wind paused. And in that unnatural stillness, she knew.

He was close.

She wasn't alone any more.

Astryd closed her eyes and inhaled, trying to steady her breath. To push down the wave of emotion rising up and threatening to swallow her whole. Frustration. Rage. And something darker.

Something deeper.
Something dangerous.

She didn't want to name it. Because if she did if she said it out loud it might destroy everything.

"I won't break," she whispered into the dark.

But when she opened her eyes, he was there. Hopps.

Only a few feet away, just as she'd known he would be. Silent. Still. Watching her like he always did not with pity, not with smug satisfaction, but with an infuriating calm that saw too much.

His eyes weren't mocking.
They weren't challenging.

They were... patient.

He didn't move.
Didn't speak.
Didn't blink.

And it made her blood boil.

"Why won't you just leave me alone?" she muttered, her voice scraping out of her throat like broken glass. It was barely a whisper. Barely enough to count.

She took a step back, her body screaming for distance. For safety. For control. Her walls rebuilt themselves on instinct, every brick laid with fury.

But Hopps didn't flinch.

He didn't shift. Didn't even raise an eyebrow. He waited. And it drove her mad.

"I told you," she snapped, louder now, voice breaking on the edges. *"I don't need you. I didn't ask for your help. I didn't ask for any of this!"* Her fists clenched at her sides. Her body shook with the effort it took not to scream.

"I hate the way you look at me," she hissed. *"Like you see something. Like I'm not just another damned disaster you're too stubborn to walk away from."*

She turned, pacing in a frantic, tight circle. The forest around them blurred. The night felt hotter. The pressure in her chest unbearable.

"You're nothing but a distraction," she spat. *"A damn distraction that's slowly driving me insane."*

She stopped. Her voice trembled.
And still she felt his gaze.

Not cold. Not sharp. Just... steady.

"You don't belong here.

Not in my head.

Not in my life.

Not in this fight."

The words were fierce. Final. But they didn't stop him. Because he wasn't fighting her. He wasn't trying to win. He was just... waiting.

She spun toward him again, fists trembling, her body shaking with the weight of what she refused to feel.

"You think your silence will wear me down?" she shouted. *"That your calm will crack me open? That standing there like some immovable force is enough to make me what? Let you in?"*

Her voice cracked hard this time. No hiding it.

"You're not going to get through to me. Do you hear me? You don't have that kind of power."

But even as she said it, she wasn't sure she believed it.

Hopps took a step forward. Slow. Measured. Certain.

Not to overpower. Not to corner. Just to be closer.

The air thickened between them. Every instinct in her screamed to run to push him back with fire and fury. But she didn't move. She couldn't.

Her breathing stuttered. Her body burned. And it wasn't just anger. It was fear.

He was getting too close. Not physically.

Emotionally. Dangerously.

And it was working.

"***Stop,***" she breathed. The word came out small. Too small.

Hopps didn't move. Didn't speak. Didn't leave. He just... stayed.

A step closer. A little warmer.
Still silent. Still present. Still patient.

Not trying to break her.

Just offering her space to fall.

And that more than anything unravelled her.

She didn't want to need anyone. She couldn't afford to.

But in this moment, as the silence between them pulsed like a heartbeat, she realized something terrifying.

She wasn't angry at him. She was afraid of what he made her feel.

What he made her *hope* for.

Finally, her shoulders slumped. Her fists loosened. Her throat ached with unsaid words.

"***Fine.***" The word cracked the air like lightning. Hopps didn't smile.

Didn't gloat. He just nodded. Once. Slow. Like he'd known this would happen all along.

The silence shifted.

No longer a battlefront.
Now... a beginning.

And in that
stillness,   Astr
yd felt it

The walls weren't broken.

They were falling.

Because
maybe
    just
maybe
        she wasn't supposed to do this alone after all.

Chapter Seven: The Quiet Push

Hopps

Hopps had been waiting for this.

He didn't need to count the days. He didn't need to keep score. The tension between them had been building since the first time she let her guard down long enough to throw a dagger illusion or not at his face. That had been her version of flirting. That had been the moment he knew.

He hadn't expected her to break easily. That wasn't Astryd's way.

But the signs were there. The micro shifts. The flickers in her eyes. The pauses in her breath when he came too close.
Hopps knew how to read the quiet.

She was fighting it resisting with everything she had. But he wasn't in a rush. He never was.

His patience was his sharpest blade. His silence, his pressure. And Astryd no matter how fast she ran was slowly reaching the edge.

She was fire. A burning, unpredictable force.
Every part of her warned people to stay away. To keep their distance or get scorched.

Hopps didn't listen. He had never been afraid of fire.
He wasn't reckless he knew the pain it could bring. He'd been burned before.

But he didn't run from it. He walked through it. He learned its rhythm. He understood what fire did when it didn't have to defend itself.

And Astryd? She was more than flame.

She was forged in it.

The sting of her defiance only deepened his resolve. It hadn't driven him away. If anything, it had only made him more certain.

Because beneath that fire, beneath the sharp words and clenched fists, was something far more fragile. Something unspoken. Hopps had seen it from the beginning.

She was guarded. Unreachable. But she wasn't impenetrable.

He had seen through the cracks she didn't know were showing. Understood the walls she'd built weren't made of steel—they were made of pain.

She hadn't let anyone in. Not really.

But what she didn't realize was that he was already inside the orbit. Already entrenched.

His presence had seeped into her life slowly. Steadily. She hadn't noticed.

Now? Now she couldn't escape it. And he hadn't said a word.

She hated that silence. She tried to fill it with anger, with denial. But it was his silence that softened her sharpest edges. That made her listen. That forced her to feel.

He didn't need to take. Didn't need to push. He just waited.

Because eventually, she'd stop fighting herself.
Eventually, she'd have no choice but to face what they were.

They were already bound by something she couldn't fight, couldn't explain, couldn't break.

She tried to ignore it. Pretended it wasn't there.

But he saw it.

In the way her breath hitched when their eyes met.
In the subtle way she tilted toward him before catching herself.
In the way she lingered just a heartbeat longer than she meant to every time they passed.

She wanted him. She didn't know it yet. But she did. And the longer she resisted, the more she unravelled.

Hopps had always thrived in quiet spaces. That's where the truth lived.

She was unravelling now. Slowly. Painfully.

Every day, a little more control slipped from her fingers. Every time he came near, she stiffened but never stepped away.

He could feel the tension coil in her when she stood too close. He could hear the war in her breath when she fought the urge to turn toward him. To let go.

She didn't want to need him. She fought the very idea. But it didn't matter. Hopps had already chosen her. She could resist all she wanted. He would be there when she stopped. And that moment was near.

They reached the river just as the sky began to bleed violet with the fading dusk. Mist clung to the surface of the water, curling in thin wisps along the bank. The current whispered secrets only the quiet could hear.

Hopps felt the shift. The way her steps slowed. The way her shoulders tensed just slightly. The way she stopped without realizing she had. Her gaze was locked on the water like it might save her. Or drown her.

She didn't look at him. She didn't have to. He was there. Across from her. Watching. Waiting.

The silence was thick but not hostile. Not between them.
This was the space where they existed.

Not in words. Not in explanations. Just in truth. And right now, the truth was this:

She was breaking. Finally. Quietly. Inevitably.

Her body stiffened again when he took a step forward not close enough to threaten, but close enough to be felt.

He didn't force her to look at him.

He simply raised his hand, and signed her name.

Astryd.

Her head turned fast her eyes locking on his like she'd been caught doing something she couldn't explain.

And in that moment, he saw it. The flicker. The truth.

It wasn't fear. It was vulnerability.

For the first time since they met, Hopps saw her. Really saw her.

Not the rage. Not the fire. Not the armor. But the girl underneath. The one buried beneath pride and pain.

The one who still wasn't sure she deserved to be seen. He didn't smile. He didn't need to. He just stood there, steady and still, and let the weight of the moment hold them both.

Then, with his hands moving slowly, deliberately he signed again:

You're not alone.

She flinched like the words had been spoken aloud. Like they cut through something deeper than skin.

Her breath caught. She looked away. Looked back. She was trying not to fall. He could see it in her posture, in the way she fought to hold the pieces together, to keep her face unreadable.

But it was too late. The cracks were there. And he had seen them. This was what he had waited for. Not triumph. Not victory. Just the truth.

She wanted to run. He could feel it. But she didn't. Not this time.

Hopps stayed right where he was. Unmoving. Unshaken. Unrelenting.

Astryd froze. The moment stretched, each second thick with tension. Her gaze locked on his, full of fury and fear and something she didn't yet have a name for.

She wanted to lash out. To scream. To say something cruel enough to make him leave. But she didn't.

Instead, her voice cracked. Her defenses folded.

"You…" she whispered. ***"You don't get it."***

Hopps didn't blink. Didn't move. He let the silence speak for him.

Because the truth wasn't in her words.
It was in her voice.
In her eyes.
In the fact that she hadn't turned away.

She couldn't deny it any more.

And neither could he.

The mission, the relic, the chaos ahead

none of it mattered in that moment.

This wasn't about the job.
This wasn't about duty.

This was about them.

Two broken souls tied together by something bigger than either of them wanted to admit.

Something neither of them asked for.

But something neither of them could walk away from.

Hopps knew it.

He had always known.

Now, she was starting to know it too.

Chapter Eight: Astryd's Decision

Astryd

The silence of the forest was suffocating.

Every step she took was marked by the crunch of brittle leaves beneath her boots. The wind moved like a ghost between the trees, threading through the branches with a hiss that sounded too much like a whisper. Moonlight sliced through the canopy in fractured beams, casting long, shifting shadows that danced on the forest floor.

And still… the world around her felt quieter than it should have.

Too quiet. But it wasn't the forest that unsettled her. It was the war inside her chest. She had given in.

The truth pulsed beneath her skin, undeniable and bitter. She hadn't wanted to admit it. Still didn't. But that didn't change the fact that somewhere between the tavern and the edge of the woods, she had stopped pushing Hopps away.

She'd let him stay. She'd let him follow. She'd let him in.

It made her stomach twist with resentment resentment not toward him, but toward herself.

She had told him a thousand different ways to leave. She'd snapped, threatened, flared magic at him like warning shots. She had made it clear that she didn't need him. Didn't want him. This was her quest. Her burden. Her reckoning.

But he'd stayed. And worse she hadn't made him leave.

Now, he was there. Always just behind her. A shadow she hadn't cast, but couldn't shake.

A constant reminder of every wall she'd failed to hold.

But it wasn't just his presence that gnawed at her. That wasn't what made her throat tighten or her pulse quicken.

It was the pull. The tension. The electricity. The magnetic thread that tied them together and tightened with every step they took.

She had given him a piece of herself. Unintentionally. Unwillingly. And yet... undeniably.

Every time she glanced his way, every time she caught him watching her with that maddening, unreadable calm it chipped at her defenses. She could feel the cracks spiderwebbing through everything she thought she had sealed shut.

She was supposed to be in control. Of herself. Of her emotions. Of her magic. But as they ventured deeper into the woods, she began to realize she was lying to herself.

She didn't want him here. She didn't need him. And yet... she couldn't imagine facing what came next without him either.

Because he saw her. Really saw her. Not just the warlock. Not just the magic. Not just the fire. He saw the woman behind it. And he didn't ask for anything. He never did. That's what made it worse.

Hopps never pushed. Never pried. Never offered comforting words or empty reassurances. He just... was. His silence was steady. Measured. Patient. A mirror she hadn't asked to look into but couldn't ignore.

It wasn't weakness. That was what confounded her most. His quiet didn't feel passive it felt like strength in its most controlled form. A quiet resistance to everything she expected from people.

He was steady, unshakable.

And she hated that she didn't hate him for it.

"Stop looking at me," she muttered under her breath, eyes fixed on the path ahead. It wasn't the first time she'd said it. It wouldn't be the last.

But, as always, he didn't answer. He didn't have to. She didn't need to turn to know he was watching her. Not in judgment. Not in pity.

Just watching. Seeing.

She clenched her fists, and the familiar crackle of magic flared beneath her skin. It hissed in her veins like lightning searching for a storm. She wanted to lash out. Set something ablaze. Anything to remind herself she was still in control.

But she wasn't sure that was true any more.

"We're not going to make it through this," she whispered.

The words carried no weight. No conviction. Just the dull echo of a fear she refused to name. She couldn't afford to be weak. Couldn't afford to let anyone see what lived behind her magic. Not now. Not this close to the end. But the longer she walked beside him, the more that fear changed shape.

Because deep down...
She didn't want him to leave any more. And she hated herself for it. When they reached the clearing, she stopped.

The trees gave way to a wide, moonlit expanse. Grass brushed at her ankles. The air grew denser, heavier, humming with magic. And beneath it all, she felt it. **The relic.**

It was close now. So close she could feel its pull, like gravity turned sideways. And still Hopps was beside her. Unmoving. Silent. Present.

"I don't want to need you," she muttered, barely audible. The words were meant for no one. A confession spilled into the air like blood from a reopened wound.

He didn't respond.

Didn't press.

He just stood, close enough that she could feel his warmth at her back. Not a fire. Not a command.

A presence. It made her want to scream. And also... to stay.

She stared ahead, refusing to meet his eyes. If she did, she feared she'd crumble. Because somehow, he'd become an anchor. And anchors could be dangerous for people who'd spent their whole lives learning how to float alone.

She couldn't afford to feel this. Not here. Not now. And yet... it was happening.

She couldn't shake him. Couldn't stop feeling him there. Couldn't stop needing the quiet way he made her feel less alone.

But she wouldn't admit that. Not yet.

"We move forward," she said, voice clipped and firm. *"We're close. The relic is near."*

Still, he said nothing. But she felt him step just slightly closer. Just enough to let her know he heard her. Just enough to remind her he was real.

And that terrifyingly he was hers to push away or pull closer.

She clenched her jaw. The path ahead was shadowed and thick with unseen dangers. Her magic stirred again, sharp and restless. A whisper beneath her skin.

Stay focused.
Stay in control.

But control wasn't what it used to be. Control was choosing to keep moving even when everything inside her wanted to stop. Control was not letting herself fall, even when the ground beneath her shifted.

"I'm not asking for your help," she snapped suddenly, needing to put the wall back up. *"You're here, but that doesn't mean I need you."*

Still, Hopps didn't react.

Didn't flinch. Just stood steady, like always. That infuriating stillness. That calm. That patience. She exhaled sharply, trying to force the heat out of her lungs.

"Let's go," she said. *"The relic is waiting."* And together, without another word, they stepped deeper into the trees.

The night closed around them. The path narrowed. And the space between them slowly, quietly began to disappear. She wasn't ready to say it. Wasn't ready to feel it. But as the forest swallowed their silhouettes, something inside her shifted.

And for the first time... She wasn't sure she *wanted* to turn back.

Chapter Nine: The Long Road Ahead

Astryd

They had been travelling for hours, and still, the relic felt as far away as when they started.

Each step seemed to take them deeper into the heart of the wilderness the trees growing denser, the air heavier with magic. The path had become less clear, the way forward blurred. The branches above had woven into a ceiling of tangled shadows, blotting out the sun and leaving only slanted fragments of light to guide them.

Astryd could feel time pressing in around her.

She was close so close. But it still felt like a dream slipping further with every mile.

As the day wore on, exhaustion crept in. The relentless pace, the constant vigilance, the magic thrumming beneath her skin—it was all wearing her down, despite the fire in her gut that urged her forward. Her limbs ached, her fingers tingled with restrained power, and the weight of the forest bore down harder with every step.

She couldn't let her guard down. Not now. Not when they were this close. And then there was Hopps. Always there. Always silent.

His presence trailed her like a second shadow sometimes comforting, sometimes suffocating. And yet... she couldn't deny the truth. Having him there made everything feel easier. The challenges. The obstacles. The long, brutal miles.

His silence grounded her, even as it maddened her. She didn't need him. But somehow, she'd come to rely on him.

She tried not to look at him too often.
She couldn't afford to.

But sometimes, her gaze would flick toward him and every time, his eyes were already on her. Quiet. Steady. Watching.

And her breath would catch, just for a moment. Because sometimes, it all felt like too much. The magic. The mission. The fight inside her. And for that flicker of a second, she wanted to give in.

But she didn't. She couldn't.

"Do you ever stop?" she muttered, adjusting the straps of her pack. Her voice wasn't angry just tired. Hopps looked at her, unsurprised. He didn't respond. He never did. But he didn't need to.

His silence spoke. In the way he moved.
In the way his gaze lingered just long enough to shift something inside her.

He was relentless. Patient. Steady in a way that unsettled her. How could anyone endure her defenses without cracking?

And yet he didn't push. He never forced anything. He just was.

And she hated that she'd begun to lean on that quiet, unwavering presence like it was a lifeline.

They walked on, deeper into the forest. The sunlight faded behind the trees, painting the world in dusk. It was the kind of quiet that clung to the skin thick and weighty. The kind of quiet that knew how to listen.

Soon, they reached a river.

The current ran swift, carving through the rocks in rhythmic rushes. The light caught the surface, turning it silver. Beautiful. Too beautiful for the chaos they were walking into.

"We'll need to cross," she said, her voice steady though her pulse picked up. Something wasn't right. She could feel it. Hopps stepped forward, scanning the current. Then he signed quick and precise. *Not safe to cross here.*

Astryd frowned. She sensed it too. The river wasn't just swift it was laced with something unnatural. Power. Old and quiet and wrong. It stirred the air in a way her magic instinctively recoiled from.

"Agreed," she muttered. *"We'll find another way."*

Hopps nodded and began moving along the riverbank, motioning for her to follow. She did. Just like always. And as they walked side by side now she noticed how naturally their steps aligned. How easily they moved as one. Neither of them spoke. They didn't need to.

It was unspoken. Unintentional. But it was happening. And it was terrifying. He was still here. Even after everything.
Even after she'd pushed and snarled and told him to leave. He hadn't.

And that certainty… it was starting to feel like something solid. Something she might be able to trust. And that? That scared her more than anything.

She forced herself to look away. She couldn't think like that. Not now. Not with the relic this close. They kept walking.

The sound of the river followed them, whispering between the trees, and the weight of the journey pressed down on her again. The relic was close,close enough to feel it in her bones. But even now, one question haunted her:

Could she truly do this alone?

Or whether she liked it or not was Hopps becoming part of her story?

The forest thickened around them. The trees towered high, their limbs tangled above like a ceiling. The path beneath them barely existed. The air grew dense. Expectant.

Hopps moved ahead, navigating the shadows with practiced ease.

And for the first time, Astryd let herself feel the pull between them.

Not physical. Not yet.

But emotional.
Something shifting.
Something real.

"I don't need you," she whispered.

But even as the words left her lips, she knew they weren't true.

Hopps didn't answer.
He didn't need to.

His silence said everything.

Chapter Ten: The Road Less Travelled

Astryd

The path was long, and the woods seemed endless.

Astryd's feet barely made a sound on the forest floor, but the rhythmic thumping of her heart felt deafening in her ears. She'd accepted the inevitable Hopps was coming with her and there was no fight left in her to push him away. The space between them was shrinking. And despite everything, she couldn't ignore the way he seemed to belong at her side, as if he had always been there.

His silence, once maddening, had become an anchor. The calm that surrounded him, the way he moved without speaking, now felt like comfort.

She hadn't asked for this. She hadn't asked for him to stay. But something undeniably tethered them together now.

The mission.

The relic.

And the quiet pull between them, one that refused to be ignored.

The trees around them grew denser, their trunks twisting upward and blotting out the sky. The air was thick with the scent of moss and earth. The silence was broken only by the sound of their footsteps and the occasional rustle of unseen creatures in the brush.

But something was different tonight.

There was a tension in the air. A stillness that felt less like peace and more like a trap.

She glanced sideways and caught sight of Hopps walking just behind her. His presence was no longer an annoyance it was... welcome. Unspoken words passed between them with every look. She could feel his gaze on her, but it didn't make her uneasy anymore.

It grounded her.

The fire that had once burned in her chest the need to fight, to prove herself strong, self-sufficient, untouchable was still there. But now, there was something steadier beneath it. A counterweight. A presence she was learning to live with.

And as much as she hated to admit it, Hopps was part of that.

"I thought you'd be the first to turn back," she said finally, her voice low but steady, breaking the silence.

Hopps didn't answer right away. He just kept walking, his presence a quiet confirmation. She didn't need him to speak. He'd followed her for days, and his silence had become part of the landscape.

She kept walking, her shoulders relaxing just slightly. The burden of her pride was beginning to slip bit by bit. Letting him in wasn't weakness. It wasn't surrender. It was choice. And it came with the quiet understanding that the road ahead was too great to travel alone.

The night deepened, but the path ahead grew clearer. They were nearing the heart of the forest, the place where the relic had been hidden for centuries. The forest itself seemed to sense their approach. The trees parted slightly, the moonlight spilling through the canopy, guiding them forward.

Astryd felt the weight of it all pressing down on her. Each step forward was a step toward the unknown. There was no turning back. Not now. Not with the relic so close. Not with danger waiting just beyond the bend.

But Hopps was here.

And somehow, that made it bearable.

"You're not afraid of this, are you?" she asked, not looking at him but feeling the shift in the air when he was near.

Hopps shook his head. His gaze was calm, but unyielding. He wasn't afraid. Not in the way she was. He didn't carry the same weight the responsibility, the curse, the pact she had made long ago.

He was a free spirit.

And somehow, that made him more dangerous than anyone she'd ever met.

But tonight, his presence calmed her.

There was something to be said for not being alone in a world that demanded everything. Something about the way he moved made the storm inside her settle, just enough to keep walking.

They walked in silence for a long time. The wind picked up, brushing through the trees in soft, eerie whispers. It was as if the forest itself held its breath, sensing their approach.

The path narrowed as they moved deeper into the woods, the trees arching overhead like twisted ribs of some long-dead creature. Moonlight filtered through the canopy in fractured silver shards, painting everything in eerie blues and greys.

Astryd slowed. The silence pressed in, heavier than before. The presence of the relic still tugged at her awareness distant, buried but it wasn't close. Not yet. The feeling was more a whisper beneath her skin than a beacon. And that uncertainty gnawed at her.

She turned to Hopps.

He met her gaze, as he always did unflinching, steady. Still silent.

"I don't know how much farther we have to go," she said, the admission tasting bitter in her mouth. *"It could be days… weeks. Or we could be walking in circles."*

Hopps didn't respond, not with words. Instead, he stepped closer not to crowd her, not to push but just enough that she could feel him beside her. Just enough to remind her: **You're not doing this alone.**

And for once, she didn't flinch away from the closeness.

She let the quiet settle between them, and when she spoke again, her voice was softer. *"You didn't have to follow me this far, you know. I gave you every reason not to."*

Hopps's only answer was a small shake of his head, then a simple sign:

Still here.

Her breath caught. Not because it was romantic. Not because it was sweet. But because it was honest. Real. And Astryd wasn't used to things that didn't come with a price.

She turned away quickly, kicking at a root with the toe of her boot. The air smelled like damp earth and the promise of rain.

They hadn't found the relic. Not yet. But they were getting closer.

And maybe… just maybe… she wasn't dreading what came next quite as much.

Because this time, she wouldn't be walking the next stretch of the road alone.

Chapter 11: Underneath the Moonlit Veil

The air in the tavern was thick cloying with the scent of spilled ale, sweat, smoke, and something else.

Something darker.

Something that curled around the spine like a whisper with teeth.

Astryd leaned against the bar, her fingers drumming a quiet rhythm on the worn wood. Her eyes scanned the dim-lit room with surgical precision. Flickering candlelight threw long, grotesque shadows against the crooked walls, each one dancing like it had secrets it refused to share. The tavern was alive in the way a haunted forest was alive watchful, breathing, waiting.

The patrons didn't notice. Or maybe they just didn't care.

They hunched over their mugs, eyes fixed on the table or the swirling contents within. Conversations flickered like dying embers in corners, murmured and broken. No one dared look too long at anyone else. That was the kind of place this was. The kind where being seen could get you killed.

But Astryd was used to being seen. She just wasn't used to being watched.

She could feel Hopps behind her.

Always there. Always just... there.

A shadow of a shadow. A breath on her neck.

It wasn't just proximity it was him. His energy. His stillness. That infuriating ability to know what she needed before she even let herself need it. Like a hand resting just beneath her ribs, holding her steady when she wanted to unravel.

It was comforting. It was infuriating. And it was starting to feel like it mattered.

Her magic pulsed faintly, her patron's whispers slinking through her consciousness like smoke through a keyhole. They never stopped. But tonight they felt more... aware. As if even they were paying attention to the space between her and the Harengon.

Gods help her, it was magnetic.

"You want something stronger?" the bartender rasped, his voice rough as the floorboards beneath her boots. He held up a bottle thick with shadow and secrets.

Astryd eyed the drink. It shimmered faintly in the dim light, dark as ink and just as dangerous.

Tempting.

But no.

"I'm fine," she said, voice low and even. The lie tasted bitter.

She turned from the bar just as Hopps appeared at her side, silent as always. He didn't speak. He didn't need to.

His hand lifted and settled at the back of her neck barely a touch. A single, grounding contact. Cool fingers brushed against her heated skin. Her entire body went rigid.

The tavern fell away.

The air between them thickened, charged. Her magic sparked in her blood, reacting not to danger, but to presence. His presence.

She met his gaze in the warped mirror behind the bar.

There it was again.

That question in his eyes.

He didn't speak it. Didn't need to.

He was waiting for her to answer something neither of them had asked aloud.

And still... she said nothing.

Not yet.

She was used to distance. Control. Walls built high and wrapped in fire. But he was steady. Quiet. Undemanding. And that quiet was chipping away at her armor like dripping water wears down stone.

"You're not going to drink it?" Hopps signed. His hands moved slow, deliberate, every flick of his fingers humming with silent tension.

Astryd gave the bottle one last glance. Her fingers twitched at her side, aching to do something.

"No," she murmured. ***"I'm not in the mood for drowning anything tonight."***

She didn't miss the way Hopps tilted his head, studying her. Always reading between lines, between breaths, between spells. The space between them felt like a held breath.

Then *bam*.

The tavern door slammed open.

The sound ripped through the air like a blade. A man stumbled in, wild-eyed, bloodshot, stinking of whiskey and something rotting.

The entire room stiffened. Conversations died.

He scanned the tavern with jittery desperation until his gaze locked on her.

"You're in danger," he croaked. And just like that, he vanished into the shadows behind him.

No trace. No sound. Like he'd never been there.

But he had.

Astryd's breath hitched.

Danger wasn't new. She'd slept beside it. Run with it. Cut it open and watched it bleed.

But this? This felt different.

Older. Hungrier.

"We should go," she said sharply, already turning. She grabbed her cloak from the back of the stool, her senses screaming. Her magic bristled at her fingertips.

But Hopps was faster.

He caught her wrist not hard, just enough to stop her. His eyes bore into hers, steady as stone.

His hands moved.

We don't know what's outside. We wait. We learn.

"Wait?" she hissed. *"You want to wait after that?"*

He didn't blink. Didn't budge.

The weight of his silence settled over her like a mantle. He wasn't forcing her. He wasn't asking either.

He was telling her.

And she listened.

Because somehow, his silence made more sense than the noise in her head.

So she nodded. Barely.

Once.

Fine. We wait.

Time crawled.

The tavern slowly returned to its previous hum, though the edges of it still felt cracked. The shadows didn't feel still any more. They felt... expectant.

Astryd stood stiffly, her hands clenched at her sides. Every instinct screamed *run*. But Hopps was beside her, calm as ever. Unmovable.

A shield without words.

And it steadied her more than any spell ever had.

Eventually, the door creaked open again.

Nothing. No man. No sound.

Just the ghost of his warning curling in the air.

"Let's go," she said softly. This time, Hopps didn't argue.

She stepped outside.

He followed.

Always behind her.

Always there.

His hand brushed her back barely a touch. But it grounded her. It *always* grounded her.

The city was quiet. Too quiet.

The kind of quiet that felt like a trap.

The kind that smelled like blood long before it spilled.

Shadows slithered across the walls like snakes, stretching thin under the moonlight. The cobblestones felt slick, like the city had exhaled something it wasn't meant to.

And between them?

The tension simmered.

That steady, slow pressure that refused to break. She could feel it pulsing beneath her ribs.

Astryd glanced sideways.

Hopps didn't look at her. He didn't have to. She could *feel* him watching.

And still… she didn't pull away.

Because something had changed.

She wasn't the one walking ahead any more.

They walked side by side.

And for the first time in her life, Astryd realized

She didn't want to do this alone.

Chapter twelve: Into the Dark

The night air grew heavier as they walked. Not just cold *weighted*. Each step felt like it pressed deeper into something unseen. Something watching.

The silence between them wasn't empty.

It vibrated. With everything they hadn't said. With the truths that hovered just behind their teeth. With the kind of tension that wraps around the ribs and dares you to breathe.

The city faded around them, buildings rising like forgotten giants, their crumbling stone faces hidden in shadow. Windows stared down at them like hollow eyes—watchful, unblinking, empty.

Above, the moon hung impossibly high. Pale silver poured over rooftops and cobblestones, making the world look dreamlike. Surreal. Like they'd stepped out of time and into something else. Something old. Something sacred. Or cursed.

Astryd could feel it. The shift. The pull.

They were close now.

Close to the relic.

Closer to the end.

And gods, the *whispers*. Her patron's voice was no longer a distant echo. It clawed at her skull now, hungry and insistent, slipping into her bones like smoke and ice.

Closer. Closer. Almost. Take it. Take it.

She winced, pressing a hand to her temple as they turned a corner. The voice retreated briefly but she knew it would return. Stronger.

But it wasn't just the magic gnawing at her sanity.

It was Hopps.

It was maddening how someone so silent could still take up so much space inside her. He didn't speak. He didn't *need* to. His presence wrapped around her like a second skin protective, suffocating, *comforting*. A contradiction she couldn't shake.

She wanted to push him away.

But she *needed* him.

And that was the worst part.

The streets were nearly empty. A rare hush draped the city like a funeral shroud. Every so often, a cloaked figure moved in the distance, drifting through the fog like ghosts. Silent. Unseen.

But Astryd felt it.

Eyes. Somewhere in the dark.

Not watching. *Waiting*.

"Keep your guard up," she murmured. Her fingers brushed the hilt of her sword familiar and worn, its grip molded perfectly to her hand like it remembered her fears.

They weren't dealing with cutpurses or petty thugs any more.

This was older. Deeper. Hungrier.

Hopps said nothing, but she didn't expect him to. His silence had always been loud enough.

But tonight...

Tonight it felt *different*.

They turned down a narrow alley, buildings pressing closer like walls closing in. The scent of damp stone and mildew thickened, clinging to the back of her throat. Water dripped somewhere, slow and steady, each drop echoing off the slick stones like a countdown.

Her heartbeat picked up. The relic was near. She could *feel* it. Not with her magic. With her *blood*. It called to her like a lover. Like a curse. A tide pulling her under.

Then the ground shifted. Her boot slid across a slick stone. Her body tilted.

Panic flared sharp, white-hot, instinctual. But before she could fall, Hopps's arm shot out. He caught her. His fingers grazed her bare arm cool and calloused against her flushed skin.

And everything *stopped*. The city vanished.
The cold, the whispers, the world

Gone.

There was only *him*. His touch. His warmth. The steady rise and fall of his breath.

Her heart was a drumbeat in her throat. She didn't move. Didn't breathe. She just *looked* at him. And he was already looking at her.

Eyes quiet, unreadable, locked on hers. He didn't ask if she was okay. He didn't have to.

She hated how much it rattled her. She hated how it *settled* her more. And that... that was the problem. The moment broke. He released her.

She straightened, every motion sharper than necessary. **"Thanks,"** she muttered, clipped.

But the softness that bled into her voice betrayed her.

Hopps nodded, but didn't look away. His gaze lingered. He didn't need to say anything. He never did. They moved forward. Deeper into the alley. The shadows swallowed them.

But the silence between them wasn't empty any more.
It *throbbed* with everything they didn't say. With every moment they touched and didn't speak. The path split. Astryd froze.

The pull of the relic was unbearable now, clawing at her ribs like something alive. Something *desperate* The left path was calling. She could feel it singing beneath her skin. But it felt wrong. Tainted.

She turned to Hopps, tension winding tight in her chest. He didn't sign. Didn't speak. But she could see it in his face.

He felt it too. The air thickened around them. Not with magic. With choice. With *change*. She felt him behind her. Not touching. Just there. Like gravity. Like a question waiting to be answered.

And for the first time...

She didn't want to fight it.

She didn't want to do this alone.

Her voice cracked like dry parchment, barely a whisper.

"I can't do this alone."

The words hung in the air like fragile glass. But he heard them. Of course he did. He stepped forward. His hand found the small of her back.

A soft touch. Just enough. Just right. He didn't sign. Didn't speak. He understood.

Together, they turned down the left path. The alley narrowed. The light dimmed. The relic waited.

And the dark rose up to meet them. But this time...

She didn't flinch. Because this time...

She wasn't walking into the dark alone.

Chapter thirteen: Fangs in the Dark

The night had grown colder as they pressed deeper into the city's forgotten veins. Buildings leaned inward, too close, their windows hollowed out like sockets in a skull. Rain from earlier still clung to the cobblestones, turning the air thick with the scent of damp stone and Mold.

Every breath felt like it belonged to someone else.
Every silence felt borrowed.

There was a heaviness now. Not just in the sky or the shadows, but in the very bones of the city.

Like the world itself was holding its breath.

Astryd moved beside Hopps, the lantern between them casting long, twisting shadows on the slick ground. The relic's pull grew tighter, every step another knot in the invisible tether wound around her ribs. It sang beneath her skin now humming, vibrating. A melody of destiny. Or damnation.

But something else stirred in her too.

A presence. Wrong. Watching. She glanced over her shoulder.

The shadows moved. Just barely but too smoothly, too deliberately. For a heartbeat, she caught the shape of a figure darting between two broken walls.

And then it was gone. She didn't say a word.

But Hopps felt it too. She could see it in the way his shoulders squared. In the sudden alert stillness of him.

Then came the footsteps. Measured. Close. *Deliberate.* Without a word, Hopps stepped in beside her, silent and ready.

Astryd's magic surged, a heat rising under her skin like a storm locked behind bone.

"*Who's there?*" she called, voice sharp as drawn steel.

Silence answered. One breath. Two. Then movement.

A figure emerged from the dark, slow and unhurried. Cloaked, hood low, face veiled in shadow. The way he walked… it was wrong. Not just confident *entitled*. His eyes glinted beneath the hood. Not with light. With intent.

"You're looking for the relic," he said, voice smooth as oil and just as slick. *"You're not the only ones."*

Astryd didn't blink. But her fingers curled toward the dagger strapped at her side.

"And what do you want with it?" Her tone was flat. Unforgiving.

The man chuckled. A cold, mirthless sound. *"Want? No, no. It's not about want. It's about what's been promised. You're playing a game you don't understand, girl. And you're not the only piece on the board."*

A chill slid down her spine, but she held her ground. Didn't let it show.

"I suppose you think you can stop me?" she asked, voice like frostbite.

The stranger's hand twitched. The air shifted. Her magic screamed in warning.

Hopps moved first, stepping half a pace forward. Shielding. His stillness was no longer neutral it was a blade unsheathed.

"Leave," the man said, something gleaming behind his smirk. *"Or I'll show you what your power's really worth."*

Then

CRACK.

A bolt of magic tore through the air, searing toward her like lightning on a leash.

Astryd raised her hand, instincts flaring. **Eldritch Blast** met the attack mid-air. The two spells collided in a shock wave of violet and gold, light blinding, force rippling out like thunder.

The stranger stumbled. But his grin remained.

"Impressive," he said. *"**Still too slow.**"*

Hopps moved in a blur. One hand swept beneath his cloak and pulled a glass sphere etched with runes. He slammed it down.

BOOM.

Shatter exploded outward. The concussive blast cracked the cobblestones, the very air screaming as sound tore through it.

The man barely got a shield up in time. Dust rose, thick and choking.

He retaliated **Magic Missile**, three glowing darts of arcane fury slicing through the smoke.

Hopps raised one hand. **Counterspell.**

The bolts unravelled mid-air disintegrating into harmless sparks. Astryd was already moving.

She sidestepped into position beside Hopps. A flick of her wrist sent a **Firebolt** hissing through the night, but the stranger spun aside fast, too fast.

"Persistent," he muttered. He drew breath and cast again this time louder. Wilder.

Cone of Cold. A wall of frost roared toward them.

Astryd threw up a **Shield** instinctively, its arcane shimmer cracking under the weight of the icy spell.

Hopps clapped his hands, whispering a curse in a tongue older than the city walls. **Sleet Storm** burst overhead. Ice and chaos swallowed the street, the enemy's vision blurred by rain and slip and disarray.

They moved as one now. Fluid. Feral. Astryd loosed another **Eldritch Blast**. The air sizzled. Hopps flanked wide, circling with surgical precision. The stranger hesitated. Just long enough.

He threw up both arms, casting **Wall of Force**, a shimmering shield arcing between them. But Astryd was already gone.

Misty Step.

A pulse of violet light. A blink. And she was behind him. He turned too late. Her next blast hit him clean in the chest.

The force knocked him off his feet. He slammed into the cobbled street, cloak flaring, smoke curling from his chest.

Silence.

He coughed, struggling up onto one elbow, cloak torn and smoldering.

Astryd stalked forward, hands still glowing, magic aching in her blood. But she didn't strike again.

Not yet.

"Who sent you?" she asked, low and cold.

The stranger looked up. His lip was split, his gaze unfazed.

"You don't get it," he whispered. *"The relic doesn't belong to you. There are forces older than your gods. Deeper than your oaths. And they're already coming."*

Her fingers curled.

"Tell me," she said.

But he only smiled.

And vanished.

Mist swirled where his body had been, dissolving like fog at dawn.

Gone. **Like a nightmare you weren't sure was real until you woke up screaming.**

The fight was over. For now.

Astryd's heart thundered. Magic still buzzed through her veins like lightning with nowhere to go.

She turned to Hopps. His cloak was torn, his breathing calm.

"You're getting better," she said, trying for something like composure. *"But we need to be faster next time."*

Hopps met her gaze.

He nodded once. Silent. Steady.

No words.

Just understanding.

They turned. Walked on.

Their shadows stretched long in the broken lantern light, curling behind them like smoke.

The relic still called.

The night still held its fangs.

And the path ahead was darker than ever.

But they weren't walking it alone.

Not any more.

Chapter fourteen: Into the Abyss

The scent of damp earth clung to the air like a second skin as they pushed deeper into the forest's maw. The path had long since ceased to resemble anything made by men. Roots clawed from the ground like broken bones, and the trees gods, the *trees* twisted upward in warped spirals, their branches reaching like skeletal hands toward a sky gone black.

There was no moonlight here. No birdsong. No breeze.

Just the thick, pulsing hush of a place forgotten by time and *remembered* by something else.

Astryd walked ahead, boots crunching against decaying leaves, but her mind drifted—back to the fight they'd just survived, to the man who vanished in smoke and secrets. There had been something in that magic. Something that *tasted* like prophecy.

They weren't just being hunted. They were being *watched*.

And the relic... it was close now.

She could feel it vibrating beneath her soles, thrumming through the roots like a heartbeat waiting to sync with her own. The magic in the air crackled around them, sparking faintly against her skin like the forest itself was testing her.

She glanced over her shoulder.

Hopps followed, one pace behind, as always. Silent. Still. His gaze was alert, flicking from shadow to shadow like he expected the trees to lunge.

He didn't speak. He didn't need to. His presence was her anchor. And for the first time she let it be.

Not surrender. Not softness. But... trust. Not all the way. But enough to matter.

They moved through the tightening gloom, the darkness pressing in until it swallowed the edges of their lantern light. Above them, the trees choked out the sky, their branches knotting into a dense ceiling of bark and bone.

Then it came.

Low. Guttural. A growl that seemed to rise not from a throat, but from the *earth* itself.

Astryd froze.

That wasn't a wolf. It wasn't any creature she knew.

It was something older. Something broken.

"Stay close," she whispered, her hand sliding to her dagger with practiced grace. The leather grip met her palm like a promise.

Hopps nodded, his expression unreadable but his body was coiled tight, every inch ready.

Another growl.

Closer now. Followed by the crack of branches under heavy weight.

And then It *emerged*.

Nearly seven feet tall, its limbs too long, its gait wrong. Fur blackened and patchy, its body hunched like it had once stood proud and had been *bent* to this shape. Eyes glowed a sickly, unnatural green. Its claws scraped the earth, and from its snarling maw came a scent of rot and arcane corruption.

A twisted fusion of wolf and something born in a nightmare.

Dark magic shimmered around it clinging to its skin like oil. It dripped from its fur in threads that pulsed with every movement.

Astryd's breath caught.

This wasn't just a creature. This was a *warning*.

A message, wrapped in flesh.

"We have company," she muttered, drawing energy to her fingertips.

Eldritch Blast flared from her hand. It struck the beast square in the chest, forcing it back with a howl.

But it recovered. Fast.

Its roar split the silence. Birds exploded from the trees only to vanish, like they'd never been real.

Hopps stepped forward, his cloak fluttering as he drew the arcane sigil into the air with swift precision.

Shatter.

A concussive blast tore through the clearing. Trees shook. Branches cracked. The creature reeled—but stayed on its feet, rage blooming in its eyes.

Then it *charged*.

Astryd cast **Firebolt**, the flames streaking across its flank. The creature screamed, but it didn't stop it only moved faster.

Hopps cast again **Sleep** and arcane light flared around the beast. It staggered...

But not enough. It snarled and surged toward Astryd.

Claws slashed through her cloak, tearing across her ribs. Pain exploded in her side, heat and blood soaking through her shirt.

She hissed. Spun. Dagger in hand, she drove the blade toward its leg but missed the artery by inches.

The beast reared back. Hopps was already moving.
Another **Shatter** rang out. The creature hit the dirt hard, chest heaving.

Astryd gritted her teeth, one hand pressed against her side, the other crackling with energy.

Witch Bolt.

Lightning burst from her fingers in a jagged arc, striking the creature mid-lunge. It screamed as the current danced across its body, violet light casting wild shadows across the trees.

Still it didn't fall.

It lunged again.

Madness in its eyes. *Hunger* in its blood. Hopps didn't hesitate. Their eyes met. *Now.*

He moved like a storm quiet and devastating. Hands outstretched, voice low and commanding. **Shatter.**

The spell detonated in the space between them, slamming into the beast with bone-breaking force.

The impact hurled the creature into a massive tree. It hit with a wet, final *crack*. And didn't rise.

Astryd stood shaking, her breath jagged. Her side burned, the wound wet and warm.

But she was still standing.

Hopps stepped between her and the beast's corpse, his hands at the ready, gaze locked. Guarding.

Waiting. The creature's body twitched once. Then again.

Then still.

Its corrupted magic fizzled out slowly, like dying embers on wet ash.

Astryd didn't exhale until the last thread of green light winked out.

Silence returned. Not peace. But the kind of silence that settles after violence.

The kind that knows this isn't over.

She winced, her hand pressed tight to her side.

"We need to keep moving," she said, voice low but steady.

Hopps didn't argue. He didn't look away from the beast until he was sure.

Then he offered his hand. No command. No assumption.

Just presence.

And she took it.

Their fingers met brief, warm, grounding.

Together, they turned from the clearing.

The battlefield behind them faded into shadow.

But ahead?

The relic called.

Its pull was stronger than ever now no longer a whisper, but a song.

And no matter what waited in the darkness...

They would face it.

Side by side.

Chapter fifteen: In the Quiet

The forest was too still.

Not the kind of stillness that came with peace but the kind that settled after violence. After blood. The kind that made every heartbeat feel too loud, too fragile.

The damp scent of the battle they'd just survived still clung to the air. Burned fur. Ash. Magic. Blood.

But the danger had passed.

And the tension hadn't.

The branches above them swayed with the wind, creaking like bones, but everything else felt frozen like the world was waiting for something. A breath. A whisper. A confession.

Astryd walked with practiced grace, but her steps were softer than usual. Her body ached with every movement. The gash across her ribs burned beneath her clothing, each breath a quiet betrayal.

But it wasn't just the pain that weighed her down. It was the aftermath.

The fight had been close. Too close. And somewhere between casting spells and dodging claws, she had felt something shift. Not in the world.

In *her*.

The realization that death had brushed its hand across her shoulder and she had *almost* reached for something other than her own strength. She pulled her cloak tighter around her body, pretending it was the cold. But it wasn't.

It was the *vulnerability*. The thing she'd spent years training herself to ignore. To kill, whenever it dared to surface.

She had prided herself on standing alone. On being the sharp edge, the survivor, the one who never leaned never needed.

And then there was Hopps. Always a pace behind. Always quiet. Always *there*.

A shadow without threat. A presence without demand.

He didn't try to fix her. He didn't try to understand her. He just *showed up*. And it was maddening.

Because she had started relying on him. On his steadiness. On the silence that didn't judge, didn't smother just *held*.

They had been walking toward the relic, yes. Toward a purpose forged in flame and fate.

But she realized now... they had also been walking toward *each other*.

And that terrified her more than anything.

By the time they reached the small clearing, her body finally gave in.

Moonlight filtered through the canopy in fractured silver strands, catching on dewdrops and moss. The world looked hushed, like a memory caught in glass.

She dropped her pack with a soft thud, boots crunching against the mossy floor. Every breath felt tighter. Her side throbbed with heat. She sank onto a half-rotted log and let herself *feel it* just for a moment.

Hopps hovered nearby. Watching. Not intruding. He never did.

But his eyes didn't leave her. That gaze quiet, steady landed heavier than any words.

She didn't look at him. Didn't *want* to need anything. But gods, she was tired.

And when he stepped forward, kneeling beside her, her breath caught.

He reached out. Fingers brushed her cloak aside, hesitating just above the wound. She flinched not from pain, but from the instinct to *refuse*.

"**Don't,**" she said, voice rough. Her pride flared, sharp as ever. ***"I can handle it."***

He didn't answer. Didn't pull away. His hands were steady. *Gentle.* He didn't press. He didn't speak. He just... waited.

And after a breath longer than it should've been she let him.

His fingers moved with quiet reverence, brushing against the blood-soaked fabric, then lifting it to examine the wound. Her skin burned where he touched her, but it wasn't from pain.

It was from *presence*.

From the terrifying truth that someone was *caring* for her, without needing to be asked. Without expecting anything in return.

She inhaled, slow and shaky. Her jaw tightened. But she didn't stop him. Not this time.

Hopps pulled a vial from his bag, uncorking it with a muted pop. The scent of herbs and something cool and minty drifted up. Healing salve. Of course he had it. Of course he knew.

She didn't thank him. Not yet.

Instead, she watched his hands. Watched how careful they were. How he moved like this wasn't routine it was *ritual*.

She had no idea what he was thinking. He never said. But somehow, she always knew what he meant.

"You don't have to do this," she said quietly, voice barely more than breath. ***"You don't owe me anything."***

He paused. Their eyes met. And in that moment, she felt *seen* completely, devastatingly seen. She hated it. And she needed it.

He didn't speak. Just went back to his task, smoothing the salve over her skin with light, deliberate strokes.

She closed her eyes. Not because of the pain. Because she couldn't hold his gaze any longer. Because she didn't want him to see the way her hands trembled.

When he finished, his hands hovered above the wound for a second longer than necessary. And then they were gone.

But the weight of him stayed. She opened her eyes, just in time to see him tuck the salve away and sit beside her. Close but not touching.

He didn't ask if she was okay. He didn't need to. For a long time, they sat in silence. But it wasn't empty. It was full of breath and stillness and something that felt like *grace*.

Astryd looked up at the sky. The stars peeked through the gaps in the canopy, soft and distant. She felt her walls creak. Not collapse. Just *shift*.

"Thank you," she whispered. So soft, she barely heard it herself. Hopps didn't reply. He just looked at her. And in his eyes she saw the truth:

I'm here. I'm not going anywhere.

The night passed like that. Two souls sitting in the quiet. Close, but not quite touching. Survivors of things they didn't talk about. Carriers of weight they didn't share.

But still together. And for the first time in longer than she could remember... Astryd didn't rest alone. She let herself believe if only for a heartbeat—that they could survive what came next.

Together.

Chapter sixteen: The Silent Bond

The day was fading.

The sun dipped beneath the horizon like a slow exhale, casting a golden haze across the tangled forest path. Shadows lengthened, stretching like reaching fingers across moss and stone. The air turned damp, thick with the scent of rich earth and blooming silence.

Somewhere in the distance, a river murmured a constant pulse beneath the hush. A reminder that the relic lay ahead. That they weren't done yet. But for now, the world had quieted.

Astryd and Hopps walked side by side, their steps nearly in perfect rhythm.

It had become second nature. The way she adjusted to his pace. The way he never overtook her, never lagged behind. The way he was just... *there*. She didn't have to look to know she could feel him beside her. A presence like gravity. Steady. Unyielding.

His silence, once maddening, had become her anchor.

She had lived her life bound to quiet voices—her magic, her patron, the old gods who whispered in her blood. She had trained herself to move alone. To carry her own weight. To never ask, never depend.

But with Hopps...

She didn't have to carry it all any more.

She didn't have to pretend she wasn't breaking beneath it.

In his quiet way, he had become her counterbalance.

When she burned too brightly, he cooled her edges.

When she doubted, he waited not with pity, not with pressure, but with *presence*.

And still... the tension simmered.

It wasn't just about the relic any more. Not just about the mission, or the danger, or what waited in the dark.

It was about *them*.

The slow, deliberate way they had begun to orbit each other. The pull that had grown between them, silent and persistent. A current she couldn't deny.

Astryd's gaze drifted sideways, catching the edge of his profile in the dying light. The sharp line of his jaw. The calm focus in his eyes. He didn't look at her, but she could tell he *felt* her watching.

She hesitated. Then said it before she could talk herself out of it.

"You're quiet today."

Hopps didn't answer right away. His eyes flicked to hers, unreadable.

Then, with careful grace, he signed: **"I'm always quiet."**

It made her lips twitch almost a smile. Almost. But there was something heavier beneath the words. Something *else* he wasn't hiding any more.

Astryd's throat tightened.

Because it wasn't just his quiet she was drawn to it was what it held. The safety in it. The understanding. The way it *let her be* without asking her to be anything else.

"I know," she said softly. **"But today… it feels different. The silence between us—it feels heavier**.

Hopps paused. Then slowly, deliberately, he signed: **"The journey isn't just about the relic. It's about what we become along the way."**

The words landed like a ripple in still water. Soft. Inevitable. She stopped walking.

Her breath caught. Her heart beat too loud in her chest. That sentence those few words hit harder than any spell, any scar. They were a mirror held up to something she hadn't wanted to name.

She looked away.

"I don't know what you're trying to say," she whispered, though part of her did. Of course she did. She just didn't know what to *do* with it. Hopps didn't push. He just stepped closer.

The space between them shrank to something impossibly small. She could feel his body heat, the quiet rhythm of his breath.

He didn't speak. Her breath hitched. The walls inside her didn't fall, but they bent. Just enough to let in the truth.

"I don't need you to speak," she said, the words barely more than air. *"I just need you to be here. With me. I don't know why… but I do."*

Hopps smiled then. Not wide. Not bright. But real. Soft. Devastating.

He signed with that same calm certainty:

"I'm not going anywhere. Not now. Not ever."

And just like that The last threads of her resistance loosened. She didn't speak. Didn't pull away.

Because the truth was, she had stopped fighting him long ago.

She had just been fighting what he represented.

Something steady.
Something true.
Something *real*.

And she didn't know how to carry that. Didn't know if she could. But for the first time… She wanted to try.

She exhaled. Slow. Deep. The kind of breath that felt like surrender not to weakness, but to something she'd never dared to believe she could have.

Above them, the forest darkened. The trees whispered to each other in the hush of dusk. The path ahead wound deeper into shadow.

The relic still called to her its presence like a drumbeat in her bones.

But tonight, that hunger didn't feel hollow. Because she wasn't walking toward it alone.

And maybe… She never had been.

Chapter seventeen: The Edge of the Abyss

The night air had turned colder. The darkness of the forest thickened with each step, swallowing the path ahead in shadow. The moonlight, once a steady companion, was lost beneath the dense canopy above.
Astryd felt the tension pressing against her skin.

The relic was close she could feel it but something else followed them. Something older. Darker. Its presence slithered behind every step they took, like a breath just behind her ear. She didn't know what it was yet, only that it was watching. Waiting.

Hopps moved beside her in silence. His presence, once an irritation, now felt essential. Steady. Expected. She hadn't thought he'd stay this long. But he had. And for once, she didn't mind.

They reached a narrow clearing. The trees parted just enough for a streak of moonlight to spill across the grass. Astryd barely had time to exhale before she heard it

A whisper. A rustle. Movement in the under brush. Her hand twitched toward her spell components. Magic prickled at her fingertips.

Hopps's fingers cut through the air, sharp and fast. ***"Wait."***
The sign hit her harder than a shout.

Astryd froze. A figure stepped from the trees cloaked, tall, eyes gleaming with quiet, focused malice. There was no time for questions.

A bolt of necrotic energy tore through the trees. Astryd reacted. Shield flared to life, absorbing the blow in a shimmer of force. The magic hissed like acid against it.

Hopps's response was immediate. **Earth Tremor** cracked the ground beneath the enemy, sending stones upward in a jagged wave. The figure stumbled.

Astryd's voice dropped to a **curse. Hex.** The spell sank its claws into the attacker, sapping him, dragging on his limbs like an anchor.
Hopps disappeared in a blink **Misty Step** and reappeared behind the enemy. **Thunderwave.** The sound shattered the stillness, hurling the figure into a nearby tree with a violent crack. Splinters flew.

Still he rose.

Astryd snarled. *"Stop hiding."* **Lightning Bolt**. Blue fire split the clearing. It hit dead centre. The figure screamed, lightning dancing across his limbs but even then, he didn't fall. Instead, he raised his hands. Darkness spilled from him like ink magical darkness, thick and suffocating.

Astryd didn't flinch. *"I see you."* **True Seeing.** The veil snapped. The world peeled back. And there he was crouched in shadow, trembling beneath the illusion. Hopps struck again. **Sleet Storm**. The earth beneath them slicked with ice, and the enemy staggered, barely keeping balance. Astryd raised her palm. **Fireball.**

The explosion devoured the night. Trees bowed under the pressure. Flame licked the edges of the clearing, painting the forest in gold and red. The attacker shrieked. Still, he stood. Desperate.

He conjured a final spell one last wave of shadow meant to shield him. But Hopps was faster. **Shatter.** The vibration tore the air. Astryd felt it in her ribs, her spine, her soul. The enemy's shield cracked like ice beneath a hammer. Astryd didn't hesitate.
"Embrace the storm," she breathed. Her patron answered. **Chain Lightning.** The sky split open.

Bolts rained down like divine judgment. They struck once twice three times. The last scream twisted into silence as the figure collapsed, limbs smoking, body twitching once before going still. Silence.

The only sound was the faint crackle of dying magic and Astryd's uneven breath. Her body trembled not with fear, but from the sheer force she had summoned. She looked to Hopps. His face unreadable.
But his eyes sharp, gleaming not with pride. Not even relief. With clarity. With the cold, steady understanding that this was just the beginning. He stepped toward her. No words. Just a hand on her arm, steadying. Grounding. The touch lasted only a second. But it anchored her.

And she realized she'd been waiting for it. ***"We need to keep moving,"*** he signed. His hands were sure. His focus locked on the fallen figure not on her. But she felt the message all the same. Not fear.
Not detachment.
But presence.
A promise.

She nodded, her chest still tight with the aftermath. ***"Right."***

They turned from the clearing. No trophies. No triumph. Just ash and questions in their wake. The relic still called. Each step toward it felt heavier. Sharper. More inevitable. They were getting closer. To something buried. Something hungry.
Something that remembered its name in blood and shadow.

The night was far from over.
But Astryd no longer walked alone.
And that truth was both her salvation
and her undoing.

Chapter eighteen: Beneath the Surface

The cold wind had begun to rise as they made their way through the narrow, winding paths of the forgotten ruins. Once-magnificent structures loomed around them, crumbling under the weight of time. There was an eerie beauty to it all a haunting stillness that only deepened the silence between Astryd and Hopps.

The pull of the relic gnawed at Astryd's thoughts, stronger now, more visceral. She could feel it in her bones, humming through the stone beneath her feet, as though the very earth pulsed with its power.

The air was charged heavy with something she couldn't name.

And still, despite the current of magic crackling just under her skin, she couldn't shake the feeling that they were being watched. The hair at the back of her neck stood on end, her fingers twitching toward the hilt of her dagger.

She glanced around, her breath fogging in the cold air but there was nothing. Only broken stone and the echo of their footsteps.

"I feel it too," Hopps signed, his expression unreadable as always.

Astryd nodded, her gaze drifting to the dense shadows stretching across the ruins. She didn't know how much more of this she could take.

The tension between them had been building an undercurrent of frustration, and something far more dangerous. Something neither of them had dared to speak aloud. She didn't know if she could face it. She'd spent too long pushing people away. But Hopps… he was different. And that terrified her more than any enemy they might face.

"We're close," she whispered, though her voice sounded small against the rising pressure in the air. *"I can feel it."*

Hopps glanced at her, his eyes narrowing. He felt it too the pull of something ancient and vast. The relic had drawn them both into its orbit, but what waited at its heart was still unknown. All they knew was that it was powerful… and not meant for just anyone.

"I still don't trust this place," she muttered. *"There's something wrong here."*

Another gust of wind howled through the ruins. The stone beneath their feet shifted.

Then a low, guttural rumble echoed in the distance, vibrating through the ground. Astryd's heart slammed into her ribs as she reached instinctively for her spell components.

But before she could react, something moved.

A blur of dark robes.
A glint of steel.
A shadow surged from the ruins like a ghost of the past.

"Not alone," Astryd growled, her voice low and dangerous.

A tall figure stepped into the faint glow of their lantern. His broad frame was cloaked, his face hidden beneath a deep hood. His presence wasn't aimless—he belonged here. His eyes gleamed with assessment, not surprise.

"You shouldn't have come," the man said, his voice sharp and cold as cut glass.

"And you should've stayed hidden," Astryd shot back, her fingers already crackling with raw magic.

Without another word, the man raised his hand and fired a blast of energy.

Astryd ducked the arcane explosion missed her by inches, but the heat of it seared past her face.

"Get ready," she breathed to Hopps though he was already moving.

A snap of her fingers. **Eldritch Blast** roared through the air, slamming into the man's chest. He staggered but didn't fall. His eyes gleamed with dark amusement.

"Foolish," he spat. *"You think you're the only one searching for it?"*

Astryd's pulse raced. No time to think. The man charged, shadows twisting around him like storm winds. Hopps stepped forward, calm and precise. He raised a hand. **Shatter.**
The blast rang out with a concussive force, slamming into the attacker's chest. Stone split. Air tore.

But the figure remained standing.

"Stay down," Astryd warned, voice like steel.

The man laughed low, cruel.

He threw his hand forward **Lightning Bolt**. The streak of white-hot power shot toward her like a blade of sky fire.

But Hopps was faster. **Sleep**, he signed, the motion sharp and commanding. The spell hit. The man froze. Collapsed. **Silence.**

Astryd let out a slow breath, trying to steady the pounding in her chest.

"You just can't stay out of trouble, can you?"

Hopps didn't reply. He didn't need to. He was already moving, scanning the ruins with sharp, silent vigilance.

She watched him. And in the flickering light, she felt it again that pull. Not just toward the relic.

Toward *him*. This quiet, constant man who had become so much more than a travelling companion.

She didn't say thank you. But she didn't need to.

"What now?" she asked, finally turning toward him.

Their eyes met for the briefest moment.

Then he signed:

"We go deeper."

And that was it.
No debate.
No doubt.

They moved forward together, their steps more certain than before.

The relic was close so close she could taste the weight of its power in the back of her throat.

The ruins whispered behind them, but they didn't look back.

This wasn't just a mission any more.
Not just survival.

They were no longer walking side by side.

They were moving as one.

And the bond between them quiet, unspoken, undeniably there was the only thing guiding them deeper into the dark.

Chapter nineteen: The Weight of Shadows

The streets were quieter now **too quiet**.
The silence pressed down on them, thick and unnatural. Every footfall was swallowed by fog, the sound of their boots on the cobblestones dampened until even that small comfort was gone.

Moonlight spilled over the rooftops in thin slivers, slicing through the mist like silver knives. The city didn't feel asleep.

It felt like it was watching.

Astryd's pulse quickened not just from the eerie calm, but from the pressure coiling tighter around her chest. The relic was close. She could feel it, tugging at her core like a hook embedded in her spine. Every step forward came with resistance, like wadding through water. The weight of it made it hard to breathe.

Hopps moved beside her, his form more shadow than man in the gloom. The tension between them hadn't lifted, but something else had settled in an unspoken understanding. He didn't try to close the space between them. He never did.

But his silence filled it all the same. And somehow, that was worse.

A rustle ahead broke the stillness.

Astryd stilled. Her fingers twitched toward her dagger. Hopps mirrored the motion—no hesitation, no need for instruction. Always ready. Always watching.

"Do you feel that?" she murmured.

He nodded once. Then something moved. A blur darted from the alley too fast to be human.

Astryd reached for her staff, but Hopps was already casting. A sharp flick of his wrist, and a **blast of force** tore through the fog, slamming into the figure mid-motion. It stumbled but didn't fall.

Astryd didn't pause. Her palm crackled with power as **Eldritch Blast** surged forward, slamming into the figure's chest and throwing it back against the stone wall.

The form shimmered flickered like a reflection in broken glass. Not human. Not ordinary. Astryd's gut twisted.

"We're not dealing with just any rogue," she muttered. *"What the hell is that?"*

Hopps said nothing. He didn't need to. He stepped forward, magic already gathering at his fingertips, a storm waiting to be unleashed.

The figure let out a low growl.
Dark energy coiled around its limbs like smoke writhing, thick with malice.

Astryd threw up a **Shield** spell. The arcane barrier snapped to life just in time as the figure lunged.

Hopps struck first. **Shatter.**

The ground buckled beneath the impact. The concussive wave blasted the enemy back again, its form distorting with the force, as if its very structure couldn't hold together.

Astryd surged forward, her dagger flashing in the gloom. She struck its arm hard. She expected bone. What she felt was wrong. Dense. Elastic. Like metal wrapped in muscle that didn't belong.

The figure shrieked, its body rippling its shape struggling to hold.

"I think it's time to end this," she said coldly.

Hopps didn't hesitate. Another spell formed in his hand a concentrated sphere of vibrating energy. He hurled it. The explosion cracked like thunder. When the smoke cleared, the figure lay sprawled across the stone, unmoving.

Astryd held her breath. Then she saw it the faint shimmer of an aura dissolving, the illusion lifting like smoke from a dying fire.

"Gone," she breathed. *"But who the hell was that?"*

Hopps stepped closer. His hand hovered near her arm not quite touching. A silent reassurance. She didn't move away.

They stood like that for a moment. Hearts still racing. The weight of the encounter pressing down harder than the fog around them.

"We keep moving," she said. Her voice was sharper now. Focused. *"The relic's close. But we're not the only ones hunting it."*

Hopps nodded, his gaze already scanning the mist for more signs of movement.

They turned back toward the path, boots echoing in rhythm again.

The shadows stretched longer.
Darker.
As if the city itself was bracing for what was coming.

But Astryd wasn't afraid.

Not any more.

They were close.

And nothing would stop her now.

Chapter twenty: Clash of Shadows

The night had grown colder as they made their way deeper into the winding, abandoned streets. The air was thick with the scent of wet stone and the whisper of wind threading through the cracked walls of forgotten buildings.

A strange heaviness lingered like the world was holding its breath.

Hopps and Astryd walked side by side, the flickering light of a single lantern their only guide through the deepening murk. The fog pressed closer with every step, like fingers wrapping around their ankles, trying to hold them back.

Astryd's thoughts were muddled by the relic's pull. With every step, its presence throbbed stronger. She could feel it gnawing at the edges of her mind, a call she couldn't ignore. But something else stirred alongside it.

A presence. Watching. Waiting.

She glanced over her shoulder. Her pulse quickened. Her hand drifted instinctively to her spell components. But there was nothing just the silence, vast and pressing, swallowing the city whole.

Hopps was silent, but his proximity anchored her. Steady. Solid. A constant she hadn't known she needed.

They turned into a narrower stretch of street, the buildings looming taller here, broken walls leaning over them like silent sentries. The fog curled thick around their feet, a suffocating veil that shrunk their world to a few feet in front of them.

Astryd slowed, squinting into the gloom. The energy humming in the air was wrong. Not the relic.

Something darker. Familiar in a way that made her skin crawl. Then movement. A shape coalesced in the mist. First a blur, then a man. Armoured. Massive. Red eyes gleaming with unnatural light. His aura crackled with dark magic, pulsing with the same hunger as the relic but colder.

"You've come far," he growled, voice distorted by the fog. ***"But not far enough."***

Astryd stepped forward, placing herself between him and Hopps. ***"Who are you?"*** she demanded.

The man drew a sword, its blade humming with restrained power.

"I am the guardian of the relic. And you are not worthy." He lunged.

Astryd reacted instinctively, thrusting her hand forward. **Eldritch Blast** cracked through the fog, striking the guardian square in the chest. He staggered but didn't fall. Raising his sword, he summoned a shimmering shield of shadow.

Hopps was already in motion. He sidestepped beside her, eyes locked in concentration. **Shatter** burst from his fingers, the sonic pulse rippling outward. The guardian's shield cracked, fractured but held just long enough for him to strike.

Astryd twisted away as the blade passed close **too close**. It grazed her arm. Pain flared, sharp and immediate. She spun back, launching another **Eldritch Blast**. This time, it struck his sword, knocking it from his grip. The guardian stumbled.

But he wasn't finished. With a roar, he hurled a **wave of dark energy**. Astryd raised a hasty **Shield**, but the force slammed into her, throwing her into a nearby wall. She hit hard, breath knocked from her lungs.

Hopps stepped forward, calm despite the chaos. He raised his hands. **Sleep**. The spell shimmered but the guardian shook it off, red eyes glowing brighter with rage.

Astryd forced herself upright, her side aching. Blood dampened her sleeve. But the fire in her chest burned hotter than the pain.

They had to end this. **Now.**

With a cry, she channelled everything she had into one focused **Eldritch Blast**. The shot slammed into the guardian's chest, forcing him back **but still he rose**.

He swung his arms wide, unleashing bursts of chaotic, destructive magic. Astryd ducked behind a crumbling pillar as the air exploded around them. *"Astryd!"*

Hopps's silent call cut through her panic. He sprinted forward, leaping over debris. Another **Shatter** exploded deafening and precise. The guardian reeled, knees buckling.

Astryd saw her moment. She broke from cover, unleashing a **barrage** of **Eldritch Blasts**, each crackling with fury. The guardian's shield sputtered, then **buckled**.

Hopps appeared behind him in a flash **Misty Step**. His fist landed square in the guardian's back, forcing him to stumble forward.

"Now," Astryd whispered.

Her hand rose, steady despite the tremble in her limbs. **One final Eldritch Blast.** It hit with the weight of a storm. The guardian collapsed. His eyes dimmed. His body crashed to the stone.

Silence.

The mist slowly receded, revealing the fallen figure. His sword lay discarded, its magic spent. The only trace of darkness left behind was a fading echo in the air.

Hopps stood beside her watchful. No words. None were needed.

Astryd's breath came hard and fast. Her fingers ached with residual energy. She stepped toward the body, eyes scanning the empty street.

"We're not done," she said. Her voice was quiet now. Tired. But sharp as ever.

The relic still called. Hopps met her gaze. Silent. Steady. They moved forward. Not just survivors now.

Something more. A force moving through shadow **together**.

Chapter twenty one: In the Quiet Before the Storm

The world outside had gone still **too still**.

The silence weighed heavily on Astryd's shoulders as she stood at the threshold of the small building, the faint flicker of the lantern casting long shadows that stretched across the room like grasping hands.

She could hear the sound of her own breath, feel the familiar weight of Hopps's presence beside her. But for the first time since their journey began, the calm unsettled her.

The relic was still out there, but the closer they drew, the more its pull began to shift. It no longer felt like a beacon of hope. Not a prize waiting to be claimed.

It felt darker now. **Hungrier.**

The weight of it pressed against her chest, stealing her breath, making her skin prickle with unease.

"We've come so far," she murmured, her voice barely more than a breath. *"But it feels like we're walking into something we can't control."*

Hopps didn't respond he never did but he didn't need to. His presence alone was enough to make her feel less alone. His gaze met hers in the dim glow, and in that silent exchange, she felt his steady support. A connection forged not through words, but through everything they'd endured together.

"You don't need to say anything," she muttered, more to herself than to him. *"I can feel you here. I'm not sure if that's a comfort or a curse."*

She'd been fighting it for so long the pull between them, the way they moved in sync without trying. They'd been so consumed by the pursuit of the relic, it had been easy to ignore. But here, in this moment of stillness, it was impossible to deny.

The quiet stretched between them, thick with all the things left unspoken. And still, she could feel him his attention on her, his steady calm seeping into her chaos. Despite herself, despite all her resistance, something inside her **softened**.

But it wasn't just him.

Something in the air tonight felt… **wrong**. It wasn't the usual hum of magic that sang in her blood, urging her forward. This felt deeper. Older. A shadow creeping along the edges of her soul.

The wind howled against the walls, rattling the windows. Her mind flashed back to the vision she'd seen earlier—twisting shadows, something watching from the dark. It wasn't just the relic calling them any more.

It was something else. **Something waiting.**

She stepped farther into the room, eyes sweeping across the worn walls, the dust-covered furniture, the flicker of lantern light dancing like ghosts. There was something oddly comforting about the space. It felt... untouched. **Safe.**
A brief reprieve from the storm looming outside.

"Hopps," she whispered, testing the stillness, *"do you ever wonder what happens when we find it? The relic. What will it really mean when we're standing there, holding it?"*

He didn't answer, of course. But he didn't need to. She could feel his response in the silence the same quiet presence that had followed her through fire and ruin. He was still here.

"I don't know if I'm ready for what comes next," she confessed, her voice barely audible. *"The closer we get, the more it feels like I'm slipping. Like the ground's shifting beneath us."*

The stillness held, heavy but not suffocating. She didn't want to be alone in it any more. Not with this. Not with everything she couldn't say aloud.

Hopps stepped closer. No words. No dramatic gesture. Just quiet understanding. His hand brushed her arm a touch so light it might

have been imagined.
But it **grounded** her.

You're not alone, he signed. *Not now. Not ever.*

The simplicity of it shattered her more than any grand speech ever could. All her walls, all the barriers she'd built to keep people out, cracked just a little more. She let out a long breath. ***"Thank you,"*** she whispered, her voice rough around the edges, the vulnerability in it surprising even herself.

Neither of them spoke after that. The moment hung between them, whole and undisturbed, until Hopps gently guided her toward the small table in the corner. He knelt at the hearth, lighting a fire that sparked to life and filled the room with warmth and soft, flickering light.

Astryd sank into a chair, her hands trembling slightly. She didn't know what the future held. Whether the relic would bring salvation or ruin. Whether it would answer her questions… or unearth new ones.

But here, in the warmth of the firelight, with Hopps sitting just across from her, she felt something she hadn't in a long time.

Peace.

The tension between them remained, but it no longer felt like a burden. It was a shared weight now.
Something real.
Something unspoken but understood.

Tomorrow, they would face the storm.
But tonight... they rested.

Together.

<u>Chapter twenty two The Edge of Desperation</u>

The landscape had shifted again less welcoming now, more jagged, more treacherous. The path they followed had become a scar across the earth, and the trees had thinned, leaving them exposed beneath a wide, unforgiving sky.

Every step forward felt like being drawn deeper into something that wanted to swallow them whole.

The air was thick with unease. The silence between them stretched for hours, unspoken yet heavy with tension.

Astryd moved like a ghost, lost in thought, and Hopps felt it in every step. He always knew when she closed herself off but this time, there was something different. Something urgent.
A pressure that pressed in from every direction.

The relic's pull was stronger now. No longer a gentle hum of magic brushing against her skin.
It was deeper. Consuming. A gnawing ache buried in her chest, urging her forward like an invisible hand pressing at her back.

But with every step, something else stirred within her.
Doubt.
Fear.

Hopps walked beside her, silent and steady. His presence alone kept her tethered. But even his calm couldn't soothe the rising dread beneath her skin.

"*Astryd,*" he signed, his fingers brushing her shoulder. The warmth of his touch sent a ripple through her. His eyes met hers, full of knowing. ***We're close. I feel it too.***

She gave a small nod, though the tension in her posture didn't ease. The relic was close and whatever awaited them beyond that final rise, she couldn't turn back now.
There was no room for hesitation.

The wind picked up cold and biting but it wasn't the chill that unsettled her. It was the sense of being watched. Of being pulled toward something ancient and waiting.

The trees vanished entirely, giving way to open, barren land and the scattered bones of forgotten ruins. Moss-covered stones lay broken across the earth, silent witnesses to a civilization long buried. The ground beneath her feet felt older than time like it remembered every secret ever whispered to the wind.

And beneath it all, that same dark hum of power, stronger than ever. Her pace quickened. She could feel it now.

The relic.

Just beyond the ridge.

Its energy throbbed through her veins. The desire to reach it burned white-hot in her blood. Hopps stayed close, his hand never far from her shoulder. He didn't have to steady her.
She was sure-footed now driven by a force she didn't understand.

They crested the rise.

Below them waited a **crumbling temple**, framed by jagged stone and a broken archway carved with ancient runes. The symbols pulsed faintly, glowing with dormant magic that stirred beneath the surface like something waking from a long sleep.

Cold wind swept through the hollow walls, whispering through broken stone.
And for a moment, the entire world seemed to hold its breath.

Hopps paused just before the steps, his hand on her arm. His gaze was fixed ahead, the shadows dancing in his eyes. *Careful,* he signed.

Astryd nodded. Her chest tightened.

The relic's energy had grown deafening. She could feel it calling not just to her, but to Hopps, too. It was in the air. In the stone. In the marrow of her bones.

She stepped forward and placed her hand on the temple door.

The stone was cold. Smooth but alive, somehow, like it had a heartbeat of its own. She hesitated.

Then, with one breath, she pushed it open. The heavy creak echoed through the stillness like a warning. They stepped inside. The darkness swallowed them whole.

Only the faintest light trickled in from the cracks above. The air was heavy. Ancient. Humming with magic so thick it pressed against their skin like water. Each breath came heavier. Every step echoed like a warning.

Hopps was just behind her, his hand brushing her back—a grounding force. He didn't rush her. He didn't speak. He just stayed.

They turned a corner. And there it was. The relic.

A crystal, glowing with eerie, otherworldly light, suspended in the air above a stone pedestal. The magic around it pulsed and swirled like a living thing ancient and powerful, aching to be touched.

It called to her.

Her hand rose on instinct, drawn toward it. Closer… Closer...

Then something flickered.

A shadow barely visible moved at the edge of her vision.

Astryd froze.

Her hand hovered in the air, **inches** from the crystal.

She turned slowly, heart pounding in her ears.

And there, standing in the doorway

Shadows clinging to his figure like smoke,
eyes gleaming with cruel recognition,
the man who had been hunting them since the beginning

was smiling.

Chapter twenty three: The Depths of Darkness

The air inside the temple was thick heavy with the scent of damp stone, moss, and ancient decay. Every breath tasted of time, like the air hadn't moved in centuries. Torchlight flickered along the walls, casting warped shadows that twitched and lunged with every step they took. The flame light danced across crumbling etchings carved deep into the stone, ancient glyphs worn by age and reverence. The walls whispered, groaned, as if breathing with ancient lungs, exhaling grief soaked in centuries.

Each footstep echoed too loud, as if the ruin itself was listening. Waiting. Every sound they made felt sacrilegious like they were walking through a grave that had never stopped mourning.

Astryd moved slowly, her pulse a steady drumbeat in her ears. She could feel it now the relic. Not just a presence, but a pulse. Like a second heartbeat that didn't belong to her, pounding in her blood, tugging at her bones. It called in a tongue older than speech, curling around her thoughts, whispering promises she didn't understand. Promises of power. Of vengeance. Of fire unbound. Promises that tempted the parts of her soul still raw from being carved open.

It terrified her. And she wanted it anyway.

She curled her fingers into fists to stop them from reaching. Just a little further. Just a little longer. Her breath trembled in her throat. The kind of trembling that came before violence. The kind that came before choice stopped mattering, and instinct took over.

Behind her, Hopps walked like a shadow. Silent, always. His steps never faltered, his gaze sweeping corners, alcoves, the long dark edges of the hallway. She didn't need to hear him to know he was tense. She could feel it in the air between them, in the way he inhaled through his nose, slow and measured. He was the eye in the storm and the blade beneath it.

The deeper they moved, the colder it grew. The warmth of the outside world vanished entirely, swallowed by stone and shadow.

Their breath steamed in the torchlight. The silence around them shifted not broken, not filled, but alive. As if the temple was aware. As if it waited. And hungered.

Astryd felt it first. That wrongness. Not loud. Not sudden. Just... there. A hum beneath her skin, like the edge of a blade brushing her spine. A tremor in the bones. The kind of knowing you don't question if you want to live. A feeling that came from somewhere beneath instinct. Somewhere soul-deep.

She slowed, lifting one hand.

Hopps stopped beside her. His fingers brushed her arm. A question.

She didn't speak. Just nodded. Her eyes locked forward.

The hallway opened into a vast chamber, roof arching high above, lost in darkness. Stone pillars lined the room, twisted and cracked, their carvings half-swallowed by creeping vines and soot. At the centre lay an altar, shattered in two. And behind it

A figure. Still. Watching.

A ripple of dread passed through her.

Before she could breathe, the sound came.

A low rumble, like thunder muffled beneath the earth. Then, the grinding groan of stone on stone. Something ancient stirring. Something waking.

Astryd stepped forward, her boots scraping against worn stone. Her fingers brushed the hilt of her staff, magic already sparking to life at her fingertips. Her chest was tight, breath shallow. Not with fear. Not entirely.

Power throbbed in her veins, dragged to the surface by the relic's call. But something else rode with it now a darkness. A taint. Like blood spilled in holy water. Like the echoes of every scream she'd ever swallowed.

The figure moved.

Tall. Cloaked in tattered robes that scraped along the floor. Its face was hidden beneath layers of black cloth, but from the shadows, two eyes flared like embers sickly orange, pulsing. As it stepped forward, the cloth unravelled like smoke, revealing skin made of ash and rot, mouthless, yet grinning. The smell that came with it was rot and sulphur, a memory of funerals she never attended.

It should not have been able to speak. But it did.

"You are too late," it rasped, voice like rust and broken bone. *"The relic is not for you."*

Astryd felt something ancient rise in her chest. Fury. Defiance. Pain. All the voices that had ever told her she wasn't enough howled in her ears. All the weight she'd carried abandonment, grief, betrayal gathered in her clenched fists. This thing thought it knew possession? It hadn't seen the rage of someone who had been broken and refused to stay that way.

She didn't hesitate.

Magic screamed from her hands, an **Eldritch Blast** hurling through the chamber, cutting the dark in half.

It hit. But not really.

A veil of shadow swallowed it, the ripple of impact vanishing like smoke in wind. The smell of sulphur and decay curled through the air. The light dimmed, as though the darkness had eaten it whole.

The figure's grin curled wider. *"You think you can take it from me?"*

Stone cracked beneath their feet as it raised one clawed hand.

The wave of power it hurled came like a storm a wall of shrieking dark that twisted the air and shattered the silence. Astryd raised her shield in time, the magic slamming into her like a fist. She staggered but stayed standing. Her feet dragged half an inch across the stone, but she didn't fall. Not again. Not this time.

Hopps moved.

Faster than thought. He stepped between them, hand flashing with sharp signs: ***We need to weaken it. Don't hold back.***

Astryd nodded, jaw clenched tight.

She summoned flame, hurling a **Firebolt** with a crack of heat. It lit the chamber in orange for one sharp moment before splashing uselessly against the shadow veil. Her breath hitched. That should have worked.

Hopps didn't stop. His hands carved power from the air. A sharp gesture, a focused breath. **Shatter.**

The temple screamed.

Stone fractured. The sound pierced the chamber, raw and violent. The figure flinched. Its barrier wavered then fractured. Not gone. But weak.

The creature hissed. And from the cracks of the temple floor, two more forms slithered out.

Ghastly, semi-corporeal wraiths skeletal limbs wrapped in strips of flickering shadow. Their movements were jagged, broken, like puppets on rusted strings. One lunged, claws stretched wide. Hopps turned, thrusting his hand forward, a streak of radiant light bursting from his palm, severing the thing in two. It dissolved into ash with a screech that clawed at their ears.

The second wraith came for Astryd.

She spun, her staff slamming across its torso. She followed with a blast of force magic that slammed it against the wall, but it shrieked and lunged again. It wrapped around her, claws digging into her shoulder. Pain flared bright and hot. Astryd growled, grabbed its face, and let lightning pour directly from her palm.

It exploded in a burst of crackling magic and dust.

But the pain stayed.

Not the wound the memory.

The sensation of hands that had hurt her once. The grip of people who took what wasn't theirs. All of that pain channelled into her next strike. This wasn't just battle. It was reckoning. It was purging. It was every silent scream given form.

The robed figure roared, voice now layered a chorus of the dead. It lifted both arms, shadows peeling off the walls like skin.
They twisted in the air, spears of pure dark aimed straight for them.

Astryd threw up a barrier. Hopps reached into his component pouch, drawing forth a gem. He crushed it in his hand, chanting under his breath. A dome of force shimmered to life around them. The spears struck, each blow shaking the dome, splintering the stone beneath.

Cracks webbed across the floor. The relic pulsed again. Louder. Insistent.

Astryd's hands lit with blue-white light.

She shouted, casting **Witch Bolt** again. The energy surged forward like a living thing, striking the creature in its chest. This time, the veil didn't hold.

The bolt punched through.

The figure reeled. Black ichor oozed from the wound. It opened its mouth too wide, too human and screamed.

Hopps leapt. He didn't wait. Sword drawn now, blade gleaming with arcane fire, he slashed across the creature's chest. Once. Twice. A third time, carving through its ribs. It fell backward, but didn't die.

It began to reform.

Astryd saw it happening. Saw the magic trying to knit itself whole.

"*NO,*" she snarled. A scream born from everything she couldn't say. From every scar carved in silence.

She called down fire.

A column of flame burst from above, engulfing the creature. Its scream turned shrill, desperate. Hopps raised both hands and cast *Shatter* again.

This time, the sound wasn't just a spell.

It was grief. It was rage. It was every broken piece of her being hurled into the abyss.

The creature's body shattered, limbs torn asunder, its face cracked down the middle. The light in its eyes flickered. Died. Its form twisted, unravelled, and with a final screech, the thing was gone. Nothing but smoldering ash.

Silence.

Astryd dropped to one knee, breath tearing through her lungs. Her body shook, nerves fried. She was covered in soot, blood, and sweat.

Hopps knelt beside her, one hand steadying her shoulder. His gaze met hers. Unspoken, but strong.

She forced a breath.

"It's here," she said, voice like gravel. ***"I can feel it."***

Beneath them, the altar glowed faintly. A heartbeat in stone.

They were not done.

But they were close.

Chapter twenty four: The Relic's Call

The air in the temple thickened with power, a static hum that vibrated through Astryd's bones. Each step forward felt like passing through a veil.

She could almost hear the relic now not a call, but a song. Clear, sharp, and unbearably beautiful. It wasn't just magic. It was a promise. Ancient. Irresistible.

Behind her, Hopps moved in silence, but even he seemed more alert, more attuned. His ever-present quiet had shifted into something deeper like he, too, was listening to something older than time. Something sacred. Something dangerous.

The corridor ended in a vast chamber. Murals lined the arched ceiling forgotten gods and long-lost battles, their paint faded and flaking like memories buried under centuries of silence. And at the far end, bathed in eerie, pulsating light, stood the pedestal.

The relic waited.

Astryd's breath caught. It was more exquisite than she'd imagined an orb wrapped in silver and black tendrils of magic, glowing with a pulse that mirrored her heartbeat. The soundless thrum pulled at her, every breath urging her closer.

She stepped forward, unable to stop herself.

The magic in the air thickened, buzzing louder, vibrating against her skin. With each step, she felt less like herself and more like a conduit drawn into the storm rather than moving toward it. Her memories blurred. Her doubts vanished. Only the need remained.

The ground trembled beneath her boots.

Her hand rose of its own accord, reaching toward the relic. The magic was alive beneath her skin. She could feel it—ready, waiting, willing.

But the shift was sudden.

The air turned cold. Shadows deepened. What had been a siren's song now felt like a command. Demanding. Hungry.

Astryd froze.

Something wasn't right.

A shape emerged from the dark tall, robed, shifting like it was made of the shadows themselves. Its eyes gleamed crimson, and when it spoke, its voice slithered like smoke around her ears.

"You're too late, child. The relic is mine."

Astryd's heart kicked against her ribs. The figure loomed impossibly tall, its presence warping the very air around it. Dark magic shimmered off its robes like heat off stone. The light dimmed in its presence. The relic pulsed harder, almost in warning.

"Stay away from the relic," she hissed, power crackling at her fingertips. *"It's mine."*

The figure laughed. The sound echoed and echoed, hollow and cruel.

"Is it? You think you can simply take it? You're a pawn. And the game is already over."

Before she could react, tendrils of shadow shot from the figure's hands, wrapping around her like chains.

They burned cold against her skin. She struggled, power flaring, but the bonds tightened, wrapping around her throat, her arms, her chest. They felt like memories. Like every voice that had told her she would fail.

"Astryd!"

Hopps moved low, fast, precise. His fingers signed with urgency:

Stay focused. We fight together.

Then: **Shatter.**

The magic slammed into the floor with a thunderous crack, shaking the chamber. The tendrils loosened. Astryd gasped, broke free, and sent an Eldritch Blast streaking toward the figure.

But it moved like liquid shadow, slipping past her magic, raising its hand again.

Hopps was there. He stepped in front of her, summoning another *Shatter*. The sound ripped through the chamber, knocking the figure off balance.

Its eyes flared with rage. **"*You dare?*"**

The floor cracked as it summoned another wave of dark energy. Shadows writhed, pulling at their feet, trying to drag them under like hands rising from a grave.

"We need to finish this!" Astryd growled, summoning fire. She launched a **Firebolt,** flames streaking through the air. Hopps followed with **Sleep**, calm and deliberate. The spell struck true the figure staggered but it shook the effect off with a scream of fury.

Its magic lashed out.

Hopps took the hit.

The blast sent him sprawling, dust and rubble exploding around him. For a breathless second, he didn't move.

Then he stirred injured but alive. His hands lifted, slow but defiant:

Still here. Still fighting.

The figure sneered, cloaked in shadow. "You are nothing but ants," it spat. ***"You think you can hold this power?"***

Astryd's gaze sharpened. She stepped forward.

"I don't need to hold it. I just need to take it."

She gathered everything rage, pain, hope, magic and let it surge. Eldritch energy exploded from her, a storm of raw force aimed straight at the figure's chest.

The blast struck like lightning.

The figure screamed.

The relic's guardian shattered its body unravelling in a vortex of dissolving shadow and crumbling power. The tendrils of dark magic disintegrated into smoke and silence.

The chamber fell still.

Astryd stood trembling, chest heaving, the echo of her magic still humming in her blood. Hopps was beside her, bruised but upright, gaze steady. He didn't need words.

They had won.

But the silence that followed was not peaceful.

Astryd turned slowly toward the relic. It still pulsed. Still waited. But the room felt different now. Heavier. Charged. Like the weight of a choice had been placed on her shoulders.

"It's over," she whispered, unsure if she meant the battle or the beginning.

Hopps said nothing. But he stood beside her. Always.

And as her eyes locked on the relic, Astryd knew truly knew that everything was about to change.

Chapter twenty five: The Relic's Power

The relic was finally in her hands.

Astryd stared down at it cool metal pressing into her palm, the etched designs glowing faintly with pulsing magic. It felt alive, as though it recognized her. Her heart pounded. Her breath caught.

And the world went still.

Everything else the chamber, the walls, the dust faded. All that remained was the relic, and the relentless thrum of power singing through her bones. The whispers were soft, seductive. Ancient. And only she could hear them.

But the moment her fingers wrapped fully around it, something shifted.

It wasn't just the relic.

It was her.

The air thickened, pressing against her chest like invisible hands. Magic surged through her veins, not as a river but a flood—and woven into that power was another presence. Familiar. Steady.

Hopps.

She turned slowly. He stood just behind her, eyes locked on hers. Silent. Focused. Unreadable. But she felt him now more than ever before. His magic. His intent. The sheer force of his attention wrapping around her like armor and fire all at once.

"You have it," he signed, his gaze holding hers.

Astryd nodded, but her fingers trembled. The relic thrummed in her grasp. Her lips parted, searching for words but none came. She didn't understand what was happening inside her. The relic had done something opened something and now every breath felt new and unfamiliar.

Then Hopps moved.

Quiet as always, but unmistakable. He stepped in behind her, hands settling on her shoulders gentle, grounding. Warm.

She stiffened.

But didn't pull away.

"You're shaking," he signed.

"I" Her voice caught. The relic's pulse blurred her thoughts, muddling words and reason. She couldn't think with him this close. Could barely breathe.

Hopps didn't wait for more.

He moved in closer, his body a solid presence at her back. One hand traced the line of her spine, slow, deliberate, until it settled at the small of her back. Not rough but not soft either. It was a touch that claimed. A touch that knew.

And it was exactly what she needed.

The magic around them swirled hers, the relic's, his all bleeding together until she couldn't tell where one ended and the next began.

"Do you feel it?" he signed, so close now that his breath brushed against her cheek.

She nodded.

She didn't know if she meant the relic. Or him. Maybe both. Maybe it didn't matter.

The room seemed to hold its breath.

His hands moved again sliding down her arms with reverent pressure, tracing fire through every nerve. She shuddered beneath his touch.

Then, slowly, deliberately, he signed: ***You're mine now.***

The words struck like a lightning bolt to her core silent, but deafening.

Her pulse stuttered. Her thoughts frayed.

She wanted to speak to resist but her body had stopped listening to her mind. The relic's power pulsed through her, fuelling the pull between them. She'd fought everything in her life. Control. Vulnerability. Need.

But this?

This she didn't want to fight.

She didn't know when the shift had happened when he'd gone from ally to something... more. But it was undeniable now. Between the relic in her hand and the man behind her, the ground beneath her had changed. She wasn't sure what this place was any more but she didn't want to be anywhere else.

Hopps's gaze softened. His hands tightened at her waist.

And in one seamless motion, he turned her to face him.

The world tilted.

His grip was firm now possessive in a way that made her knees weak. His breath was warm against her lips. His eyes burned with a heat that made her forget everything else. The relic pulsed harder. So did her heart.

I won't let you go, he signed.

The words weren't just a promise.

They were a vow.

And Astryd, for the first time in her life, didn't want to run.

She felt it now what the relic had unlocked wasn't just magic. It was surrender. Not weakness. Not fear. But choice.

She had no idea where this path led.

But with Hopps holding her steady, she was finally ready to follow.

Chapter twenty six: The Tethered Path

The sun had long since vanished beyond the horizon, casting the world in shadows thick enough to swallow sound. Silence stretched in every direction wide, oppressive, complete. The night clung to everything, draping the ruined temple in a hush so total it felt like the air itself was holding back.

They stood in the aftermath, the relic between them, its hum of magic still pulsing like a heartbeat. But the weight in the air wasn't just from the relic's power. Something else lingered something heavier. A tension neither of them had dared name.

Astryd felt Hopps close behind her, his presence like gravity steady, inescapable. He didn't need to speak for her to feel his focus, the way it wrapped around her like a tether. She was used to solitude. To command. To silence filled only by her own breath and the echo of her steps. But now, with the relic in her hand and his shadow at her back, she wasn't sure where her autonomy ended… and his influence began.

For a long moment, neither moved.

The world held its breath. So did she.

Hopps's silence, once a balm, now felt like a pressure on her chest. She could sense his gaze steady, unmoving. Not hungry. Not demanding. But certain. Unshakeable. The kind of certainty that didn't ask it claimed. And beneath it, something inside her shifted, tugged loose from the walls she had spent years building.

She turned, her gaze locking with his.

She didn't know what she expected. Reassurance, maybe. Distance. But what she saw instead was something possessive not cruel, but inevitable. Like a decision had been made long before she knew there was a choice. A truth that had waited patiently for her to catch up.

The relic throbbed in her grip, its magic laced with something colder now. Something more aware. As if it, too, had been waiting.

"Astryd," Hopps signed slowly, his fingers grazing her arm light enough to be respectful, firm enough not to be ignored. ***Trust me.***

Two words. But they landed like a command.

Trust was not something she gave freely. She had survived by keeping others at arm's length, her magic honed like a weapon to keep the world from getting too close. It was easier that way. Cleaner. But here, in this moment, everything she'd built to protect herself felt like it had been slowly and deliberately dismantled.

She didn't respond. Couldn't. Her throat tightened around words she didn't have, her breath catching between defiance and need.

Hopps's hand lingered on her arm. Not forceful. Not possessive. But claiming all the same. His gaze was unflinching. His stillness a challenge she didn't know how to answer.

I'm not going anywhere, he signed again. A vow. An anchor. A dare to let go.

Astryd's heart hammered against her ribs. She wanted to deny the shift between them, to retreat into the safety of strategy and magic. She wanted to armor herself in the lies she'd told to survive. But the ground beneath her had already tilted and he hadn't let her fall.

She took a shaky breath. ***"I don't need you,"*** she whispered, but her voice betrayed her. Too soft. Too uncertain. It wasn't the lie that cracked her it was the way it rang hollow in her own ears.

He didn't flinch. Didn't rise to the bait. Instead, he stepped closer, his hand reaching up to trace the edge of her jaw so gently it nearly undid her.

She tensed.

Not because she feared him.

But because she didn't.

And that frightened her more than any battle ever had.

Without a word, he closed the distance between them, pulling her into his arms not possessively, not gently, but with intent. Steady.

Absolute. Like he knew she could break but believed she wouldn't.

The silence deepened around them.

He didn't whisper reassurances or offer platitudes. He didn't need to. His grip said enough: ***You're mine. And I'm not letting you go.***

Astryd exhaled shakily.

She could have pushed him away.

She didn't.

She stood frozen, caught between instinct and desire, between control and surrender. Her body taut with the tension of wanting and fearing the same thing.

Her magic still simmered beneath her skin, but it was no longer shielded. Not from him. The walls she'd built to keep herself safe had cracks now and through them, he slipped in like moonlight.

She didn't know when it had happened
When the line blurred.
When partnership became entanglement.
When the fight turned inward.

But she knew, without question, that this he was no longer a variable she could dismiss.

Her voice was a whisper now, almost lost to the silence. *"This isn't who I was supposed to become."*

Hopps didn't react.

He only held her tighter, one hand resting at the base of her spine like a brand. Not to restrain her. To remind her.

You are now, his silence said.

And for the first time, she didn't fight it.

She breathed him in.

And let herself stay.

Chapter twenty seven: A Shift in the Air

The morning after the relic had been claimed, the world seemed quieter. The air felt different, as if the earth itself had exhaled a breath held for centuries, now finally released.

The wind stirred gently through the trees, brushing against the leaves like a sigh of relief, as if nature itself had witnessed the chaos and now settled into tentative stillness.

Astryd stood at the edge of the camp, staring into the forest beyond.

The relic rested in her palm, its magic pulsing in time with her heartbeat. Each pulse sent a shimmer of energy through her fingertips, a reminder that it was no longer just an object of power. It was part of her now bonded, fused, changing her in ways she had yet to understand. Her hand tingled with its warmth, and yet, it felt like holding the weight of something ancient and alive.

Behind her, Hopps lingered. She could feel him, as she always did. He had become a constant, his presence woven into the rhythm of her life like the subtle beat of a war drum. They had travelled in silence since the battle, but the space that had once existed between them had vanished. It had disappeared the moment the relic had chosen her.

Now, it wasn't just the magic that tugged at her centre. It was Hopps steadfast, silent, and impossibly sure. His nearness was a presence in her bones, something that grounded her when her own thoughts became too loud.

She had spent her life in command of herself, her choices, her fate. But with him, control no longer felt like a necessity. It wasn't surrender it was balance.

Hopps didn't demand obedience or speak in declarations. He didn't need to. His quiet presence held a gravity she couldn't ignore. A force that steadied her in the chaos, that pulled her back when the tide of her power threatened to drown her.

The rustle of leaves behind her didn't startle her. She already knew he was there. She knew what he would do next. His steps were measured, deliberate, as he approached and brushed his hand against hers. The contact was brief, but it steadied something inside her anchored her to the now.

She turned to face him, eyes locking with his. His expression was unreadable, as always, but there was something new in his gaze an unyielding calm, a restrained intensity. She saw no judgment. Only certainty. He didn't waver. Not once.

Hopps signed, *We're not done yet. There's more to face.*

Astryd gave a slow nod. Her pulse thrummed, not from fear, but from the undeniable truth blooming between them. The relic had awakened something in her but so had he.

She had spent so long resisting connection, wearing her strength like armor. But now? She didn't want the armor. Not with him. Not any more.

Her hand lifted to touch his arm tentative, questioning and he didn't pull away. The moment deepened, and she felt it: the undercurrent of something unspoken. Trust. Power. A strange, dark tether neither of them had asked for but both had accepted. It hummed between them like a shared pulse.

The fight for the relic was over. But the real reckoning was only just beginning.

She exhaled, her voice low. *"What now?"*

Hopps didn't answer aloud. Instead, he took her hand and held it, grounding her in the moment. His fingers were warm, sure. His eyes softened. *We continue,* he signed. *And we face it together.*

They resumed their journey, but the path ahead no longer felt the same. Every step was different now charged not just with magic, but with shared purpose. The air around them crackled faintly, as if the world itself could sense the shift between them.

That night, they camped by a quiet stream, the fire crackling between them. The silence was no longer filled with unspoken doubt but with something steady, mutual. They didn't need to talk. Their bond had outgrown language. Words would only cheapen what had already been said without speaking.

In the quiet hours that followed, Astryd leaned into the weight of what they'd become.

Not lovers.

Not strangers.

Something forged in shadow and trial.

Something irrevocable.

She sat beside him, shoulder brushing his.

No words passed.

None were needed.

Hopps's silence had once felt like distance. Now, it was the thread pulling her forward. A silent promise. A vow sealed not in sound, but in presence.

She had once believed that power came from solitude. That strength meant standing alone. But now, sitting beside him beneath a sky streaked with stars, she realized something else:

Sometimes strength was found in surrender not of will, but of isolation

Whatever came next, she would not face it alone.

And that more than the relic, more than magic was the real shift in the air.

Chapter twenty eight: The Weight of Choice

The sun had long since dipped below the horizon, leaving the sky a dark canvas punctuated by a scattering of stars. The night air was crisp, and the faint rustle of the forest whispered secrets only the ancient trees could understand. It was as though time had slowed, offering a rare moment of peace amidst the chaos that had defined their journey.

Astryd stood at the edge of the campfire, staring into the flames. The relic pulsed in her hand, its power echoing the rhythm of her heartbeat. Each beat felt amplified now, as though her blood no longer belonged to her alone. It was no longer just an object of magic it was a part of her. And like everything else she'd claimed in her life, it came with a price.

She could feel Hopps behind her silent, steady. His presence had always been constant, but now it felt different. The distance she'd once clung to had vanished the moment the relic chose her. And with that shift, everything else had changed too.

Hopps's silence no longer offered comfort alone. It held weight now, a quiet command wrapped in restraint. It was the kind of control that didn't need to be spoken, and it was beginning to unravel something inside her. It was a tether she hadn't asked for but couldn't deny, a stillness that called to something deep and buried in her.

She glanced over her shoulder. He sat near the fire, cross-legged, his gaze fixed on her. The flickering light danced across his features, casting shadows that only deepened the mystery of him. He hadn't spoken much since they'd left the ruins but then, he never did. And yet, she could feel him everywhere. Like a presence sewn into her breath.

The pull between them had intensified since she took the relic. It wasn't just magic any more. It was him. The way he moved with quiet certainty. The way he looked at her like he knew her better than she knew herself. She'd been in control for so long, but something had shifted—and she was starting to wonder if she wanted it back. Or if she even could.

She felt frayed. Powerful. Unmoored.

"Astryd," Hopps signed slowly, his hands fluid in the firelight. *What's troubling you?*

She swallowed hard. The words caught in her throat. How could she explain the war inside her? How could she admit that she was afraid not of the relic, not of the path ahead but of what it meant to trust him? To lean. To be seen.

"I don't know," she murmured. *"I've spent so long fighting for control. Leading. Surviving. But now..."*

Her voice trailed off. She didn't finish the thought. She didn't have to. The weight of it lingered between them, heavy and sharp.

Hopps's gaze didn't waver. He signed again, steady and sure. *You don't have to fight any more. I've got you.*

The words hit her harder than she expected. Not because they were sweet but because they felt like a challenge. He wasn't offering comfort. He was offering something more dangerous: the option to let go. To stop clawing for control. To hand over the reins.

And she wasn't sure she knew how.

She looked away, her fingers tightening around the relic. It pulsed again, but she barely felt it. All she could think about was the weight of his gaze. The stillness of his hands. The unrelenting steadiness that made her feel like she didn't have to hold everything together alone. That maybe, just maybe, she didn't want to.

"I don't know if I can do this," she whispered. *"I don't know how to let go."*

He didn't flinch. Didn't blink. Just reached for her hand, his fingers steady as they brushed against hers. *You don't have to do it alone.* His eyes locked with hers, and in them, she saw no hesitation. No doubt. Just a promise.

We do this together.

Together.

The word echoed through her. And for once, it didn't feel like weakness. It felt like freedom. Like finally breathing after a lifetime of holding her breath.

She had built her walls high, made them thick and impenetrable. But now, with him, they felt less like defense and more like a cage. A cage she had locked from the inside.

She rose to her feet. Each step toward him felt like crossing a boundary she'd once vowed never to breach. But she crossed it anyway. Every part of her screamed to retreat, to armor up. But something louder a truth blooming quietly in her chest urged her on.

He didn't move.

Just held out his hand.

She took it.

The connection hit her like a storm quiet, sudden, powerful. It wasn't just a touch. It was a shift in gravity. A surrender not of strength, but of isolation.

We face it together, he signed again, unwavering.

Astryd nodded, the tension breaking in her chest. Her voice cracked with softness. *"Okay,"* she said, barely more than a breath. ***"Okay. We will."***

For the first time in years, she didn't feel the need to lead. She didn't feel the need to fight.

And for the first time, she was ready to follow not because she was weak, but because she trusted the one beside her to never let her fall. She was not alone. Not any more.

Whatever came next, they would face it. Together.

And together, they would not break.

Chapter twenty nine: The Stillness That Waits

The woods had grown too quiet.

Astryd noticed it first the way the usual rustle of branches and calls of distant night creatures had gone still. No wind. No life. Just silence, deep and unnatural, like the earth itself was holding its breath.

She stood near the remnants of their small fire, the relic resting against her chest like a second heartbeat. It pulsed in slow, deliberate waves. Not urgent… not yet. But present. Watching. Waiting. Each throb felt like a countdown, a measured warning from something ancient and unseen.

Hopps was nearby, crouched near the edge of the tree line, his sharp eyes fixed on the shadows. He hadn't moved for a long time. Neither had she.

It was as though the world around them was suspended in time. As though something someone was watching. Not passively. Not curiously. But with intent.

Astryd shifted uneasily. Her magic felt... different tonight. Not unstable, but heavy. Muffled, like it was being held down by unseen hands. Even when she tried to summon a flicker of flame between her fingers, the spark sputtered and died. The silence swallowed it. She tried again, slower this time. The flame bloomed, weak and reluctant, and it cost more than it should have.

The relic wasn't feeding her power. It was hoarding it. Drawing it inward. Preparing.

"Something's wrong," she said, barely above a whisper. *"I can feel it."*

Hopps turned toward her, his face pale in the firelight. He signed slowly, *I feel it too.*

Then, after a pause: *We're being watched.*

Astryd stiffened.

She wasn't imagining it. That cold pressure at the base of her neck, the hairs that refused to settle. The sense of something ancient and merciless just out of view. Something that didn't need to be seen to be known. It was a presence that pressed in around them like a closing fist.

"We shouldn't stay here."

Hopps nodded in agreement. But neither of them moved. There was nowhere safer. Whatever waited for them whatever had been stalking their steps since the ruins would come, no matter how far they ran.

She turned from the fire, the shadows behind her too long, too thick, like they were bleeding out from the trees.

She walked toward Hopps slowly, the relic pulsing heavier now, as if it were responding to the presence in the forest. Her fingers curled around it, tight. The metal was warm, too warm, like it had been feeding on her own heat, her own fear.

Hopps reached for her hand not to hold it, not quite. Just a grounding touch. Reassurance. Anchor.

But when their eyes met, Astryd saw it the flicker of something behind his calm.

Fear.

Not panic. Not dread. Just a silent, controlled knowing. He was ready to face what was coming, but he wasn't sure either of them would survive it. And that truth lingered in the stillness between them like smoke before fire.

The fire behind them hissed, though there was no wind.

A low sound too low to be a voice rumbled from somewhere deep in the woods. A groan, almost. Like the earth shifting under strain. Like the breath of something buried beneath the surface.

Astryd's breath caught. *"What was that?"*

Hopps didn't answer. He was already rising, drawing closer to her, protective. He glanced to the relic. Then to her.

It wants something.

It's not done with you.

Astryd shook her head. "***Then it'll have to wait.***"

But even as she said the words, she knew she was lying. The relic had stopped waiting long ago. It had chosen her. And soon, it would claim her in return.

She turned to Hopps and whispered the question neither of them had been brave enough to ask before.

"What if I can't come back from this?"

Hopps stared at her.

Then signed, slowly

and with finality:

Then I'll go with you.

A silence stretched between them.

Not a heavy one.

A resolute one.

Astryd exhaled, the weight of her fear pressing down on her chest like stone. Her hand tightened around his, as if to memorize the shape of it, the promise of it.

In the distance, something moved a shape passing between trees. No sound. Just the ripple of fog, twisting unnaturally where it shouldn't. It shimmered at the edges, barely there. But it was coming.

Hopps reached for her hand again, and this time she let him hold it. Fully. Without hesitation.

They didn't sleep that night.

The stillness held.

And far beyond the firelight, something began to wake.

Something that had waited long enough.

Chapter thirty : The Final Stand

The night had never been so cold, nor had the world around them ever felt so unforgiving. The moon hung low in the sky, casting a sickly glow over jagged rocks and twisted trees. Everything was still unnaturally still. The kind of stillness that only came before something terrible, before the sky split or the earth screamed.

The air was thick with tension, heavy with the weight of something ancient and waiting.

The relic pulsed in Astryd's hand, its power growing stronger with every passing moment. She could feel it deep in her bones, not like a whisper, but a scream under the skin calling her forward, urging her toward something she couldn't yet see but knew was waiting, like her name had been carved into fate itself.

Hopps walked beside her, as silent as ever, a steady constant. But something had shifted in the days since they'd claimed the relic. They no longer felt like two separate entities he was part of her, and she was part of him. Every step was in sync, every movement tethered by something deeper than magic. Something sacred. Something terrifying.

But tonight, the air was different charged with doom.

They had come too far to turn back.

The path narrowed ahead, the trees thinning into a clearing. Astryd's breath caught in her throat. The hairs on the back of her neck rose. The relic pulsed faster, as though it sensed what was coming. Shadows twisted unnaturally, and the fog crept in like a living thing, thick with malice.

And then, the silence shattered.

A figure stepped from the mist tall, cloaked in tattered black robes. Their face was hidden beneath a hood, but glowing eyes pierced the gloom like twin embers pulled from a funeral pyre. The air around them distorted, bending like heat waves. Reality wavered.

"I've been waiting for you," the figure said, their voice deep and grating, like stone on stone. It carried something old, older than the relic itself. A hunger wrapped in prophecy.

Hopps moved instinctively, protective, hand resting on his weapon. The figure's presence cloaked the clearing like a curse given form.

"You think you can keep it?" they sneered, voice thick with contempt. *"The relic doesn't belong to you. It belongs to my patron. It always has."*

Astryd didn't flinch. *"No one owns the relic,"* she said coldly. *"It chooses. And it chose me."*

The figure laughed, the sound hollow and cruel. *"Then it chose wrong."*

A wave of black energy exploded from their outstretched hand. The air crackled, tendrils of dark magic curling toward Astryd and Hopps. Astryd countered immediately, her **Eldritch Blast** cutting through the gloom. But it struck a shield of dark energy, rebounding in a shock wave that shook the ground.

The battle began.

A jagged blade of pure shadow shot from their hand. Astryd twisted, but it caught her shoulder, tearing flesh. She hissed in pain but stayed standing. Hopps launched **Shatter** with a deafening crack, momentarily staggering the enemy.

Astryd surged forward. She cast **Firebolt** after **Firebolt**, twin arcs of flame lighting up the darkness. Each blast was met by a deflection or twisted into something else entirely. But she didn't stop. Her magic roared through her veins she was relentless, driven by fury and purpose and a quiet, buried fear.

The figure retaliated with a sweeping arc of shadow magic that split the earth beneath them. Astryd leapt over a crevasse, rolling mid-air and landing hard, knees buckling. Her palm slammed into the earth as she used it to push herself up, sweat and blood streaking her face.

"I won't give in!" she shouted, breath ragged. She threw her arm forward, summoning a streak of crackling lightning. It struck the figure's side, blasting their form with raw energy. The figure howled but rose again, smoke curling from their robes.

She moved like fury incarnate blades of arcane energy forming in each hand, slicing through the fog. She closed the distance, darting, dodging, attacking in a flurry. The figure parried with shadows, countered with necrotic blasts. Their power twisted the very air around them.

She was fighting for her life.

And for a time, she was winning.

She ducked, rolled, spun beneath a sweep of dark magic that would've torn her in two. Her hands danced through sigils, stringing spell after spell together. Ice and fire. Force and thunder. Her magic was a storm of will and fury.

Then her body began to fail.

She was burning too fast, drawing too deep. Her breath came in ragged gasps. Her limbs trembled. But she kept going.

The figure saw it the crack in her stamina and struck.

Dark tendrils erupted from the ground, binding her wrists and ankles, dragging her down. She screamed, fire bursting from her hands, burning the bonds away but not before a second jagged blade of energy slashed across her thigh.

She collapsed.

Blood pooled beneath her. Her cloak torn. Her magic flickering.

Still, she crawled forward, one desperate hand in front of the other, dragging her broken body toward the relic where it had fallen. Her fingers brushed its surface. Power surged into her again wild, desperate.

She forced herself upright.

She cast **Eldritch Blast. Firebolt. Shatter.**

The clearing lit with blinding, chaotic force. The enemy's shield cracked, their robe scorched. For one fleeting heartbeat, they faltered.

And then finality.

A burst of magic, vile and seething, blackened the sky and air alike. It struck her in the chest before she could summon a defense.

Pain bloomed searing, world-ending pain.

Astryd's scream echoed across the valley.

The relic slipped from her fingers.

Her body crumpled.

And everything went black.

Hopps's POV

The world shattered in an instant.

Hopps saw it all unfold in slow motion. He had seen enemies fall before, comrades die in battle. But this this was different.

Astryd, the one who had been by his side through everything, crumpled to the ground as if all the life had been drained from her.

His heart stopped. His breath froze in his chest.

No. No, no, no.

His feet moved before he even realized it, his body rushing to her side, his hands trembling as he cradled her in his arms. Her face was pale, her eyes closed, her chest no longer rising and falling.

"Astryd!" he whispered, his voice breaking.

He pressed his ear to her chest, hoping praying against all logic that he would hear something. But there was nothing. The world was too quiet. Her body was too still.

The sound of the figure's laughter echoed in the background, but it was a hollow noise, distant. Hopps didn't care. He didn't care about anything but her.

"*Astryd...*" he whispered again, his voice choked with grief. "*No. Please, no.*"

His fingers gently brushed over her skin, feeling the coldness that had already begun to set in. He felt the power of the relic still pulsing weakly, but it wasn't enough. Nothing was enough.

Her body was so cold.

So lifeless.

And he was powerless to do anything.

Hopps's chest heaved as he looked at her, helpless, devastated. He had failed her. He had promised to protect her, to keep her safe, and now she was gone.

No.

This wasn't the end.

The fury that had always simmered beneath the surface surged up, hotter than it had ever been before.

His grief twisted into rage. He didn't care about the relic any more. He didn't care about anything but making them pay.

The magic that had always been a part of him flared to life, surging like wildfire through his veins. He had never felt such raw, unrestrained power.

The air around him crackled as he called upon everything he had, the earth beneath him trembling in response to the destruction he was about to unleash.

He stood, clutching the relic to his chest, but it wasn't enough. Nothing was enough.

With a guttural cry, he unleashed a wave of magic, the force of it sending shock waves through the ground. The figure before him faltered, but it was too late. Hopps had already reached them, the magic flowing from his body in a torrent of destruction.

Shatter.

The figure's shield cracked like glass, disintegrating under the sheer force of Hopps's magic. The ground trembled as everything around them seemed to fracture and collapse.

Hopps didn't stop. He couldn't stop. He needed to make them pay. Every ounce of pain he felt, every ounce of fury, poured into the destruction.

The figure staggered back, eyes wide with fear, but it was too late. Hopps's magic slammed into them with the force of a tidal wave, ripping through their dark energy, shattering their defenses.

The figure screamed as they crumbled to the ground, their form disintegrating into nothingness, vanishing under the weight of Hopps's wrath.

Hopps didn't care.

He was still lost in his grief, his anger,

his desperate need to make them pay for taking her from him.

His body trembling,

Hopps dropped to his knees beside Astryd's lifeless form.

His hands shook as he cupped her face, his tears falling freely as he whispered her name over and over again.

"Astryd... please... don't leave me," his voice was raw, his words breaking like waves crashing against the shore.

He stayed there for what felt like an eternity, unable to move, unable to think. The relic pulsed between them, but the world was too dark, too silent, and the only sound that remained was his heart, shattered beyond repair.

Chapter thirty one: Surrounded by Shadows

The air was no longer still.

Hopps felt the shift before he saw it. Not in the trees, not in the fog but in the weight of the world around him. The battlefield lay silent, scattered with the broken remnants of enemies turned to dust. And Astryd

Her body was still. Too still.

The sight of her broken frame ripped through him like a blade plunged into the centre of his chest. Her face, so fierce in battle, now lay slack with the silence of death. Her lips parted slightly, as if she had one last word she never got to say. Her eyes were closed not peacefully, but like a door slammed shut. Hopps's hands hovered over her chest as though afraid to touch her, afraid to confirm what he already knew.

But the grief couldn't take him yet.

He clenched his jaw against the sob rising in his throat. There would be time to fall apart later. Maybe. But not now. Not while shadows still stirred. Not while her name still echoed like a ghost in the air.

His hands were bloodied, trembling as he lowered her gently to the earth. His knees dug into the broken soil as he leaned close.

"I'm sorry," he whispered, voice cracking, each syllable torn from somewhere far too deep. *"I should've stopped it. I should've protected you. I should've been faster. Stronger. Anything but this."*

And then he heard it.

A rustle. A whisper of cloth. The cold breath of more monsters to come.

He forced himself to his feet, not because he had the strength, but because he couldn't stay kneeling beside her not with the storm that was coming.

From the shadows, they emerged.

The first figure stepped out from the mist, eyes glowing like coals in a dying fire. Others followed, cloaked in tattered robes, their bodies humming with dark, familiar energy. A second wave. Worse than before. They moved with purpose, circling like vultures drawn to blood. Like predators smelling weakness.

Hopps's pulse thundered in his ears. His magic was nearly gone, his hands already shaking with the weight of too many spells. But rage was a fuel all its own. And his was not quiet.

It roared.

"You can't save her," one sneered. *"She's gone. And now, you will be too."*

Hopps's hand tightened around the relic. The pulse was faint, but it answered him. One beat. Then another. Echoes of her. Echoes of *them*.

"No," he growled, voice low and full of fire. *"I won't let her die in vain."*

They rushed him.

"SHATTER!"

The word tore from him like a battle cry, like a prayer too loud for gods to ignore. The blast erupted outward like thunder, flattening the first two attackers in a violent shock wave of flame and fury. Hopps's eyes blazed. Fire surged around his arms as if the very elements had heard his pain and answered.

He spun, casting **Firebolt, Magic Missile** his voice rising into a roar with each strike. Each spell was a scream. Each flare of light a howl of vengeance. He was no longer just fighting. He was *avenging*.

A blade of shadow slashed across his ribs. He staggered, screamed, but the pain only stoked the blaze within him. He reached for the fire again ripping it from the air, from the ground, from the hollow place in his heart.

"BURN!" he snarled, hurling a Fireball that exploded in a blaze of rage, reducing three figures to cinders. The flames reflected in his eyes. He was no longer casting spells he was channelling wrath incarnate.

The fog thickened, more enemies slipping through its shroud. Hopps let out a primal scream and cast **Shatter** again. The pulse sent bodies flying, the earth cracking beneath their feet. Blood and smoke filled the air. His knees buckled but he refused to fall.

Blood poured from his wounds now, soaking into his cloak. His arms shook from the recoil of his own fury. But he didn't care. Not when they had taken *her*.

The enemy leader stepped forward, tall and cloaked in shadows, power radiating from him like a storm ready to swallow everything.

"You think you can stop us?" he said, his voice mocking. *"Look at you. Broken. Alone."*

Hopps bared his teeth, eyes blazing with grief sharpened into hate. *"You're already dead."*

With a final scream that split the sky, he threw everything he had left into the relic.

The air detonated.

The blast cracked the earth wide open, hurling the leader backward in a maelstrom of flame and ruin. Shadows disintegrated. Lightning split the sky. The battlefield lit like a sun had risen inside it and then went still.

Hopps collapsed.

He was done.

His chest heaved. His limbs refused to move. The enemies were gone or maybe not. He couldn't tell. It didn't matter.

All he could see was her.

"Astryd…"

He dragged himself to her side. Pulled her into his lap. Cradled her face with hands that trembled, not from pain, but from everything breaking at once.

Her skin was still cold.

"Please…"

He was sobbing now. Broken. Utterly undone. The kind of weeping that tore itself from the soul. The kind of grief that didn't sound human. That didn't *want* to be.

And then the relic pulsed.

Not weakly this time.

Strong. Purposeful.

He looked down.

The hum vibrated through his hands, through her body. Not chaotic. Not violent. But *focused*.

And in the stillness of the ruined battlefield, with ash in the air and blood on his hands, Hopps held his breath.

Waiting.

Hoping.

Bleeding for a miracle.

Because he had nothing left to give

Except *her*.

Chapter thirty two: The Weight of Despair

The battlefield was dead.

Not quiet dead. The fog had thinned, but something worse had taken its place. An echo, a weight, a suffocating stillness that pressed on Hopps's chest like stone, each breath dragged through the ash and ruin like a blade across bone.

Magic clung to the air in thick, rotting strands. Smoke curled from shattered ground. The smell of burnt blood and scorched shadow lingered like a curse carved into the air. It crawled under his skin, filled his lungs, coated his tongue with iron and soot, until every breath tasted like death.

Bodies or what was left of them lay scattered in the dirt. Blackened bones. Ash. Ragged cloth stained with magic and grief. There were no cries, no moans, no gasps for breath. Just the aftermath.

His enemies were gone.

But so was she.

Hopps knelt in the centre of the ruin, cradling Astryd's body like something sacred, like a relic more powerful than any he'd ever known. Her skin had gone grey. Her lips blue. Her braid was undone, tangled with dirt and blood. Her armor cracked and burned. Her hands, once curled with defiance, now hung limp.

She looked peaceful.

And that gods, that broke him most of all.

She was never meant to look peaceful. Not her. Not the firestorm in the shape of a woman who never bowed, never yielded. She should've gone down screaming, teeth bared, magic burning the world around her. But instead she had slipped away in silence.

He hadn't even been able to give her a peaceful death.

His hands trembled as he brushed the hair from her face, his voice nothing but a rasp. **"*You were supposed to live through this*,"** he whispered. **"*You were supposed to come back with me.*"**

But she didn't move.
Didn't breathe.
Didn't fight.

And the silence screamed louder than any battlefield ever could.

The relic pulsed weakly in his hand, its rhythm erratic. Fading. Drained. Useless.

He didn't care.

He wanted it to die too. To crumble into dust like the hope it once carried. He wanted the whole world to break with him. To feel the ruin churning in his chest.

Hopps pressed his forehead to hers, his tears falling freely now. His shoulders shook with the effort to contain what no man could hold in the grief that split mountains, the agony that shattered stars.

He'd used everything. Burned every shred of his magic. Fought until his bones cracked and his skin tore. Until the ground itself had bled with him.

And none of it had been enough.

The rage had left him hollow. The vengeance had tasted like ash. And now, he was just a man kneeling beside the corpse of the one person he couldn't live without.

He let out a broken sound, low and guttural. Something between a sob and a scream. It ripped from his chest like it was tearing muscle from bone, raw and animal. A sound that belonged to someone who had lost everything.

"I failed you."

The words hit the ground like blood. Thick. Final.

He didn't notice the figures until they shifted in the mist.

Eyes. Dozens of them. Watching. Waiting. Glowing like the embers of every fire he hadn't lit.

They didn't move closer. Not yet.

But they were there. Standing in the fog like sentinels of judgment. Like death in the shape of men. Like grief come to walk.

Hopps didn't move.

What was the point?

He had nothing left to give. No magic. No fight. No hope. The war had cost him everything. And the victory? If you could call it that was as hollow as the ache in his chest. The kind of ache that lives in bone and shadow and never lets go.

The relic hummed again. Just once.

He barely noticed.

His arms curled tighter around Astryd's body, shielding her from the cold. Shielding her from the wind that cut like glass. He didn't know why. Maybe part of him still believed she could feel it. Maybe part of him still thought warmth would call her back.

"I'm sorry," he whispered again. *"I should've been faster. Stronger. I should've known it wasn't over. I should've known..."*

He could feel the exhaustion pulling at him, dragging him under like an undertow. He was bleeding he knew that. Magic-burned. Shredded from the inside out. But it didn't matter.

He could die here.

That would be fine.

Let the shadows take him. Let the world go dark.
Let the pain finally end.

But the figures didn't strike.

They just stood.

Waiting.

Circling.

And that was worse.

Hopps forced himself to lift his head. His jaw clenched. His muscles screamed. Every tendon felt like it might snap from the strain. But he looked up because if he was going to die, he would look death in the eyes.

"You want me?" he rasped. *"**Then come get me.**"*

But they didn't move.

The fog thickened around them, swirling like smoke around bone. Their shapes were barely human. Their faces blurred. But their eyes glowed. Patient. Predatory.

And Hopps empty.

He sank lower, his body giving out beneath the weight of his grief. His knees hit the ground with a thud that echoed in the bones of the world. The relic slipped from his fingers and rolled into the dirt beside them.

Still glowing. Still pulsing. But he didn't reach for it.

His hand just hovered, trembling in the air between them.

"Astryd…"

Her name was a gasp. A prayer. A plea. His breath hitched. His vision blurred.

And then nothing.

No more words.
No more strength.

Only silence.

And the waiting.

Chapter thirty three: The Unleashing

The fog still swirled around them, thick and suffocating. The air hummed with a charged energy, the remnants of the battle hanging like a heavy mist over the land.

Hopps sat on his knees, grief-stricken, cradling Astryd's lifeless form. His heart bled with despair, the weight of his failure almost too much to bear. He had done everything but it still hadn't been enough to save her. The silence around them was cruel. Mocking.

His fingers clenched around the relic, his only hope now, his only prayer, as the faint pulse of magic flickered weakly within it like a heartbeat struggling to continue.

"Astryd..." His voice trembled as it broke through the silence. *"Please..."*

And then, as if the universe had finally answered his desperate plea, a pulse of power shot through the relic. It was a quiet tremor at first, a flicker in the stillness, like the first inhale after drowning but it grew. Stronger. Brighter. It swelled into something undeniable, something ancient.

Astryd's chest rose.

A breath.

Then another.

Hopps's breath hitched in his throat, his hands shaking as he held her close, his body straining to believe what was happening. His heart thundered. His vision blurred.

Her skin flushed with colour. Her body warmed beneath his touch. Her muscles, limp and lifeless, began to tighten with strength.

Her eyes snapped open, cold and wild.

There was no confusion in them. No weakness. Only fire. A fire that hadn't been there before. A fire that had been forged in the void.

"Astryd..." Hopps whispered, his voice trembling with relief, but also awe. Terror. Reverence.

This wasn't the same woman who had fallen.

She was more.

She was death.

Without a word, Astryd pushed herself up, her movements sharp, dangerous, effortless. Her limbs coiled with power. Her eyes—no longer the eyes of a mortal swept over the battlefield like a goddess assessing her dominion.

She was no longer just Astryd, the warrior she had been before.

She was something else.

Something far darker.

Something unstoppable.

She felt the power surging through her raw, unfiltered magic that tore through her like wildfire. The relic, still in her grip, pulsed with insatiable hunger, feeding her, empowering her, transforming her.

Her gaze flicked to Hopps. For a heartbeat, her eyes softened.

But the next? Ice. Steel. Wrath.

"Astryd...?" Hopps asked, his voice rough with disbelief, reverence lining every syllable.

She didn't answer with words.

She answered with power.

The ground beneath them shook as she stood. Magic exploded from her like a detonation, a wave of energy rolling outward, hot and ruthless. Her body crackled with violent magic, every fiber of her being alive with destruction.

She raised her hand, and the remnants of dark energy in the air recoiled like prey sensing the arrival of the apex predator.

The enemies who had once circled Hopps—who had thought him weak, easy looked upon her now.

And for the first time, they hesitated.

They had been foolish.

Astryd's lips curled into a smile, but it wasn't kind. It was carved from vengeance, seared with fury. A smile shaped by death.

With a roar, she unleashed her power.

A wave of destruction rolled out from her like a tidal wave. The earth trembled. Cracks tore through the ground. The storm she had become erupted in full.

The fog didn't stand a chance.

It scattered like ash on the wind, shredded apart by pure magical force. The first wave of enemies were vaporized no scream, no fight. Just gone.

Her magic moved like a tempest. Fire roared, lightning danced, shadow twisted and broke. It wasn't chaos it was command. It was fury guided by will.

She turned on the next group, her gaze frozen and merciless. They tried to summon shields, conjure wards of dark magic but they shattered the moment her power touched them.

With a flick of her wrist, lightning split the sky, tearing through bodies and soul alike. Their forms disintegrated, turned to ash and ruin. Astryd moved like a blade through a battlefield, slicing clean through doubt and mercy.

She stomped through the field, boots crushing bones and embers. Each step thundered like a drumbeat of finality.

She wasn't just defending. She was erasing.

Erasing everything that had ever dared to threaten them.

Her body glowed with magic. Her skin pulsed with arcane force. Every inch of her burned with power too great to contain, and she didn't try. She let it bleed out in waves that tore through the land.

"No one will harm him again," she hissed, her voice low, feral, the growl of a storm given form.

Hopps stood back, heart pounding. Breath frozen. Eyes wide. He had known power. He had known terror.

But he had never seen this.

Astryd was a maelstrom. A god wrapped in mortal skin. Her fury could end empires.

When the last of the enemies fell, when there was no more movement, no more threat, the battlefield fell silent once more but it was not the silence of death.

It was reverence.

The dark magic that had filled the air was gone. Replaced by the echo of her wrath.

Astryd turned to Hopps, her eyes still burning with fury and something more.

Something deeper. She was no longer just the woman he had loved.

She was legend.

"*Are you still with me?*" she asked, her voice like thunder held back by will alone.

Hopps nodded, throat dry, soul shaking. "*Always,*" he whispered, voice hoarse, carved with awe, drenched in devotion.

Astryd's gaze softened just slightly. She stepped toward him. The relic pulsed between them, a reminder of what had been given and what had been taken.

This wasn't just survival any more.

This was evolution.

"*Then let's finish what we started,*" she said, her smile like lightning on the edge of a storm. And as the ruins of war smouldered behind them, they turned, side by side.

The world would know now

Nothing. Not death. Not shadow. Not fate itself could take what was *theirs*.

Chapter thirty four: Rebuilding the Empire

The battle had ended, but the war within still raged. As the dust of the conflict settled, the desolate landscape stretched before them a battlefield of death and shattered remnants.

The once-pristine grounds were now scarred by the violence that had torn through them. Blood-stained earth, charred bodies, and the lingering echoes of destruction painted a grim portrait of the cost of their survival.

Hopps stood motionless, staring out at the wreckage. His clothes were torn, his body bruised and battered, but it was his spirit that seemed most broken. The price of victory had been higher than he ever imagined, and the cost was written in the empty spaces where friends once stood, the silence that hung in the air, and the weight of Astryd's power that still loomed over him like a shadow.

Beside him, Astryd was a stark contrast. Where Hopps was quiet and somber, she was a force of nature tired but unyielding. Her fiery gaze scanned the horizon, her mind already working through the implications of their actions.

Her magic still pulsed through her, a constant reminder of what she had become. Her resurrection had come with a price, but now, it was time to rebuild. Time to make it all mean something.

The relic, still glowing faintly in her hand, seemed to resonate with a hum that filled the empty space around them. It had not only brought her back to life but had enhanced her power beyond what anyone could have predicted. But with that power came responsibility something she didn't yet fully understand, but knew she would have to.

"We can't stay here," Hopps said, his voice low, cracked from battle and grief. *"We need to get the others together. There's still work to be done."*

Astryd didn't look at him. Her eyes were fixed on the devastation, her thoughts running deeper than words. She knew the battle was only the beginning, and the real struggle was yet to come.

"I know," she murmured. *"We can't undo what's been done. But we can stop it from happening again."*

Hopps turned to face her, noticing the coldness in her voice. It wasn't like before. She wasn't the same woman who had fallen in the fight there was something darker within her now. The magic, the raw power she had absorbed, had changed her in ways impossible to predict.

"How do we fix this?" Hopps asked, his voice strained. He had never felt more helpless. He had always been the one with the answers, the strategist. But now, standing beside Astryd, he felt like he was fumbling in the dark.

Astryd finally looked at him. Her eyes were sharper, more focused than ever, but there was a hardness to them. *"We rebuild. But we rebuild stronger. We gather the pieces of what we have left and form something greater than what we lost."*

She clenched the relic tighter in her hand, the power within it responding to her touch. *"There are still those out there who will want to see us fall. And I'm not letting that happen. Not again."*

The weight of her words hit Hopps hard. He had seen her angry before, but this was different. This was vengeance, cold and unrelenting. And it scared him. She had been resurrected, yes, but at what cost? Would the woman he had known still be in there, beneath the magic, beneath the fury?

"Astryd…" Hopps began, his voice soft, hesitant, *"Are you sure you're ready for this? After everything that's happened... after what you've done…"*

She didn't let him finish. She took a step forward, standing taller, stronger, the weight of her power seeping into her very presence. *"I have no choice, Hopps. We have no choice. We either rebuild this empire or watch it crumble to dust. And I won't let that happen. Not again."*

Her voice was fierce, commanding, and it left no room for doubt.

Hopps's heart clenched. He understood. She was no longer the same person she had been before the fight, and maybe she never would be. The lines between her humanity and her power had blurred, and there was no turning back. But despite the fear that gnawed at him, he knew one thing for certain: he would follow her, no matter what.

"I'll follow you," he said, his voice firm, resolute. *"But we need to move quickly. There are still those who will challenge us. And we need to prepare for what comes next."*

Astryd nodded. *"I'll lead. But we do this together."*

With that, they began to gather what was left. Hopps reached out to their remaining allies, sending word to those scattered across the lands, calling on old friends, former allies, and those who would stand with them. The remnants of their army, though shattered and broken, were still alive, still breathing. And with them, they would rebuild.

As they moved through the ruins, Hopps's eyes occasionally flickered toward Astryd. Her expression was unreadable, but her steps were sure. She was stronger than ever before, and there was no mistaking that. But deep down,
Hopps couldn't shake the fear. Fear that she might lose herself to the darkness, to the very power she had absorbed.

But there was no time for doubts. There was no time to ask what had changed in her. The world was still broken, and they needed to fix it. Together.

They would rebuild, and in doing so, they would create a new empire one forged from the ashes of their losses. The weight of the world was heavy on their shoulders, but for the first time, they were not alone.

And that was enough.

For now.

Chapter thirty five: Rebuilding Their Intimate Dynamics

The rebuilding process wasn't just about the physical world around them. It was about restoring the delicate balance between Astryd and Hopps the unspoken bond that had always existed, a thread of quiet understanding woven through chaos and war. But now, after all they had endured, that bond had changed. It hadn't broken.

It had deepened.

But deep didn't mean easy. It meant uncharted. It meant full of things left unsaid of touches not yet taken, of truths too raw to voice.

The moon hung low, casting a pale silver glow over the shattered remnants of their camp as the broken edges of their world began to settle. Fires crackled low. Distant conversations faded to murmurs. The air was cold, not with winter, but with aftermath. The kind of stillness that comes after a scream. After a resurrection. After too much.

They had survived. But survival had its cost.

Astryd had returned stronger than ever, touched by something ancient and unknowable. The magic that now pulsed within her was raw and wild, coiled under her skin like an unsleeping beast. It was power, yes but it was also weight. A burning stone on her chest. A voice that never stopped whispering.

She didn't say any of this. Not out loud. She didn't know how. But the way she stood now too still, too rigid told the story for her.

Hopps noticed. He always did. The way her eyes lingered on the horizon too long. The way she breathed in quick, shallow pulls like she was afraid to take up too much space. Like she didn't trust her own lungs any more.

She'd died. Come back. Taken on the kind of power most people feared even in nightmares.

And Hopps? He had watched her fall. He had screamed her name with blood on his hands and begged the stars for something anything to bring her back. And when she had opened her eyes again, burning with a light he didn't recognize, he hadn't known whether to thank the gods or curse them.

Now, here they sat. A fire between them. The night heavy with the weight of everything unspoken.

"I can't carry it alone," she said at last.

The words were quiet. Barely there. But they cracked the silence wide open.

Hopps didn't hesitate. He didn't blink. he signed **"You don't have to."**

Simple. Unshaken. Truth wrapped in warmth.

She didn't answer. Not right away. Her throat tightened, jaw clenching against the emotion swelling beneath her ribs like a rising tide. She wasn't someone who admitted fear. Or weakness. Or anything, really.

But here, under the stars, she didn't want to lie to him.

So she let herself lean just the faintest tilt of her body against his shoulder. Her armor didn't clatter to the ground. Her magic didn't rebel. She didn't fall apart.

She just... breathed.

And Hopps stayed still. A steady presence, warm beside her. His shoulder pressed gently into hers, solid and safe. He didn't move. Didn't speak. Just allowed her to exist in the quiet, without demand or expectation.

Her voice cracked when it came again. *"I'm scared I'm not the same."*

"You're not," he replied gently. *"None of us are."*

She turned slightly toward him, searching his face in the firelight. She expected doubt. Pity. Distance. But what she found instead was calm. Steady eyes. Soft breath. A man who had seen her at her worst and had never looked away.

"But you're still you," he added, *"And I'm still here."*

She didn't realize she was crying until the first tear slid hot down her cheek.

He noticed. Of course he did.

His fingers brushed hers, tentative. Not claiming. Not pushing. Just asking.

And she let him. She turned her palm and slid her hand into his. The contact was simple. Human. Real. Her magic didn't flinch at the closeness it pulsed gently, like it approved.

That small connection said more than any words.

She didn't need to be strong tonight. She didn't need to lead. Didn't need to carry the weight of the relic or the empire or the fear that she might burn too hot and lose herself again.

She just needed this.

So they sat there in the stillness, letting the night settle around them like a blanket. Stars hung above, soft and ancient. Wind rustled the trees. The fire popped and crackled. And inside that silence, something mended. Not loudly. Not completely. But enough.

Later, when the fire had burned low and the shadows stretched long across the tents, Hopps rose and offered her his hand.

He didn't say anything.

He didn't need to.

She took it.

His fingers curled around hers not with force, but with promise. With trust.

They walked side by side into the shelter of canvas and starlight, the world outside their tent forgotten for just a little while. Inside, the night held only warmth. Shared breath. The soft hush of limbs folding close.

They didn't speak as they lay down.

They didn't need to.

Her head found its place on his chest, his heartbeat a steady lullaby beneath her ear. His arms wrapped around her, and her body melted into his like it had always belonged there.

There were no barriers between them now.
No roles to perform.
No weapons between their ribs.
Only two souls finding their rhythm again.

She whispered his name once. Just once. And he answered her not with a declaration, but with a thumb brushing the curve of her cheek, tucking a loose strand of hair behind her ear like it mattered.

And it did.
Because love didn't have to be loud.
Sometimes, the fiercest declarations were made in silence.

As she finally drifted into sleep real sleep, unguarded, unwatched Astryd knew this wasn't just rest.

This was freedom.

Not from battle.

Not from destiny.

But from the loneliness that had lived inside her bones too long.

She had returned from death.
But it was here, in the hush of this night,
in the safety of his arms,
that she truly came back to life.

They would rebuild the empire.
They would face the battles to come.
But tonight, they rebuilt the most important thing of all

The sacred, unshakable tether between them.

Gentle.
Steady.
Unbreakable.

Chapter thirty six: The One Who Always Finds You

The morning broke slow and gray. Ash still clung to the horizon, smoke curling from the smoldering remnants of the battlefield. The air hung heavy with loss, with things unsaid and undone. Astryd stirred beside Hopps beneath the thin canvas shelter, the warmth of his arm still around her.

But there was a new tension in the air familiar, yet changed. It coiled low in her gut, humming against her bones like a memory returning too soon.

A quiet hush spread through the camp, like the earth itself holding its breath.

And then, the sound of heavy footfalls.

Measured.
Calm.
Unshaken.

A figure stepped through the tree line, cloaked in pale mist and wearing the soot of a thousand battlefields. Her silhouette carried no urgency, yet the weight of her presence shifted the air. The fog parted for her. The light bent around her. She was a wound and a balm in the same breath.

Dragonborn. Ravenite. Cleric.

She carried no weapon, but the weight of her presence could bring an army to stillness.

Blu.

Astryd stood slowly, the movement stiff and automatic, her shoulders instinctively tensing until her eyes met the cleric's. And in that moment, she didn't see a stranger. She saw salvation in scales. Safety wrapped in storm light. Her body remembered before her mind did.

The world tilted then steadied.

"*You came,*" Astryd whispered, voice raw with disbelief, thick with something dangerously close to hope.

Blu smiled not wide, not boastful. Just enough. The kind of smile you give someone you've carried in silence, across worlds, and back again. The kind of smile that says, *Of course I did. I always will*.

"You're not easy to lose, Astryd," Blu said, voice smooth, deep, edged in warmth. *"Not even in death."*

Hopps rose beside her, cautious at first, his eyes narrowing. But something in his posture eased the moment Blu met his gaze. There was no posturing between them. No challenge. Only mutual respect, carved from shared scars and quiet understanding.

"You always show up just after the storm," Hopps said quietly.

"Because someone has to rebuild the light," Blu answered.

Astryd took a step forward, but her legs nearly gave out. Blu caught her before she could fall, hands strong and sure, as if she had been doing it for a lifetime.

She held her like someone who had never let go.

"You held me once," Astryd murmured, her voice cracking like old stone. *"In the dark. I remember it now."*

Blu didn't flinch. *"You broke, and I stayed. You burned, and I knelt beside you until the flame made room for breath."*

Silence fell, thick and aching.

Hopps looked away not out of obligation, but reverence.

Astryd wrapped her arms around Blu, pressing her forehead against the cleric's scaled shoulder. It wasn't weakness. It was refuge. It was remembrance.

"You saved me," she said, voice small. *"More than once."*

Blu exhaled slowly. *"And I always will."*

They stood like that for a long moment a warrior reborn, and the cleric who refused to let her fall. Not even death had severed that bond.

Later, when the sun began to rise in earnest, Blu knelt at the centre of the ruined camp. Her presence anchored the space. Survivors gathered. No speeches. No ceremony. Just quiet gravity. She radiated peace, even as the ground still smouldered beneath their feet.

One by one, they came to her.
Not just for healing.
For grounding.
For clarity.

She offered no absolution.
Only grace.

And when Astryd took her place beside her, Hopps at her back, it was clear something had shifted again.

This wasn't just the rebuilding of an empire.

It was the rebuilding of a heart, a bond, a hope made flesh.

Blu became the quiet strength among them. The one who steadied shaking hands. The one who remembered names, whispered truths when silence became too loud. Her magic was powerful, yes but it was the way she *stayed* that undid people. The way she listened like their pain mattered.

She helped mend what battle had broken not with spells alone, but with the kind of stillness that left people different. Better.

At night, when fires flickered low and the stars blinked overhead, Blu sat beside Astryd, telling stories from older days some made up, some not.

And Astryd laughed.

Not the strained, polite sound of survival.

The real kind.

The kind that rang through the camp like a song no one remembered they needed.

Blu didn't demand answers. She didn't question what Astryd had become. She simply accepted her power and pain, shadow and fire and reminded her that even gods bled once. Even gods needed friends.

In a world torn open, Blu was the thread pulling it back together. Quietly.

Unshakably.

Without fanfare.

She didn't just find Astryd.

She reminded her she was never truly lost.

And Astryd, for the first time since rising from the dead, began to believe it.

Chapter thirty seven: The One Who Knew Her Before

The fire had died low. Most of the camp slept or sat in silent recovery, wrapped in their own quiet griefs. But Astryd was not resting.

She paced beyond the outer warding runes, alone, her fingers twitching like they couldn't forget the weight of destruction. She had burned the world back to life. But the cost still echoed in her bones. Her magic still simmered beneath her skin unsettled, humming with the residue of death and resurrection.

And Blu, Blu watched her from the shadows. Not as a guardian. Not as a priestess. Not even as a friend. But as the only soul left who remembered the girl beneath the wreckage. The version of Astryd that laughed before she led. The one who bled before she burned.

She waited.

Until Astryd sank down beside a crumbling stone, knees drawn to her chest, her face hidden in her arms.

Only then did Blu step forward.

She didn't speak. She didn't touch. She just sat. Beside her.

The silence stretched long, like it had no end. Like it had always been there between them, waiting for this moment. Heavy with things neither of them had said because they'd never needed to. Not until now.

"I don't know who I am," Astryd said at last, voice barely louder than the wind.

"You do," Blu said softly. *"But right now, you're afraid of her."*

Astryd's shoulders trembled. *"What if she died?"*

"She didn't," Blu replied, calm as moonlight. *"She's just buried. And not by magic, or war. But by grief."*

Astryd looked up, eyes rimmed red but dry. *"You speak like you've done this before."*

"I have." Blu turned her gaze to the horizon. *"I've been the buried one. And the one who dug."*

Astryd didn't speak, but her posture eased just enough for truth to slip through the cracks.

"You always saw me, didn't you?" she whispered.

Blu didn't hesitate. *"Before anyone else. Before even you did."*

A long pause. And then*: "Why?"*

"Because I knew what it meant to burn," Blu said, her voice low. *"And I saw the way you carried the match in one hand... and a prayer in the other."*

Astryd let out a hollow laugh. *"There's no prayer left in me."*

"Then let me pray for you."

That shattered something.

Astryd curled in on herself, and for the first time since her resurrection, she wept not with rage or power but with release. The kind of cry that sounded like surrender. The kind that only someone who had carried too much for too long could ever truly understand.

And Blu moved not to fix. Not to offer platitudes. But to sit behind her, arms circling her shoulders, holding her steady like roots hold the storm. No force. No pressure. Only presence.

"Do you remember," Blu said gently, *"the first time you asked me to teach you to heal?"*

Astryd nodded, eyes shut tight. *"I sliced my palm open on accident. You didn't even flinch."*

"I held your hand and said, 'Pain isn't weakness. It's a reminder that we're still here.'"

"You always had a way of making it make sense."

Blu leaned her head against Astryd's. *"And I always will. Because you're worth making sense of."*

They sat like that for a long time. No grand declarations. No epic turning points.

Just a woman being held. Just a heart allowed to tremble without consequence. Just truth.

"I'm scared of what I've become," Astryd admitted.

"**Then let's meet her together,**" Blu replied. ***"Not with judgment. With grace."***

Astryd exhaled, the breath shuddering from her lungs like it had waited an eternity to escape.

She didn't have answers. But she had this. She had Blu.

And not far from the edge of the firelight, Hopps stood in the shadow of a crooked tree, watching.

He hadn't meant to intrude. He had followed only to keep her safe. But what he saw froze him not in fear, but reverence. Astryd, strong and burning and broken, held by someone who asked nothing of her. Who knew her not by title or legend, but by soul.

Hopps's chest tightened. He saw her pain, raw and unguarded. Saw the trembling in her hands. The weight in her eyes. The love she couldn't name.

And he saw Blu not trying to take it from her. Not trying to heal it away. But simply holding it with her.

It was the kind of love that expected nothing in return.
The kind of love that made space.

He wanted to run to her. To fall to his knees and promise that she didn't have to carry it alone. But in that moment, he knew

This wasn't his to fix. This wasn't a wound that love could close by force. It needed to be honoured, not solved.

He lowered his head, eyes burning, and signed her name *"Astryd."* it didn't reach her But maybe, somehow, the feeling did. He stepped back, silent, letting the shadows claim him again.

But his heart carried the moment like flame. He would not forget. And neither, he knew, would she.

Chapter thirsty eight: Aftermath

The morning after was quiet.
Not peaceful, peace hadn't touched this place in a long time but quiet in that hollow, sacred way that comes after devastation. The kind of quiet that felt like the land itself was holding its breath.

Ash still clung to the edges of the camp. Smoke curled upward from fire pits and shattered tents. The ground bore the scars of everything they had survived magic, blood, sorrow. It was ugly. Raw. But the fires were out, and the living were still breathing. That counted for something.

Hopps stood near the edge of the warding stones, hood drawn low over his eyes. He hadn't slept. Not really. Not after what he'd seen. Not after her.

The images played in his mind on a loop, seared into the backs of his eyes like brands: Astryd unravelling in the dark. Blu holding her with a silence that spoke more than any words could. No incantations. No light shows. Just two arms wrapped around a soul that had nothing left to give.

And him?
He'd watched from the shadows. Silent. Useless. His silence had once been a balm, but now it felt like a cage. For the first time in his life, his love hadn't been enough. His loyalty. His protection. None of it had mattered when the dam inside her finally broke. He couldn't reach her.
But Blu had.

Hopps pressed a gloved hand to his jaw, trying to ground himself. The ache in his chest didn't ease. He hated how grateful he was. Hated how much it hurt. Because he'd sworn to be the one who never let her fall.

But some things… some things you couldn't catch.
Some things you could only witness.

Behind him, the camp stirred. Not fast. Not loud. Just enough to remind him the world hadn't ended. Not yet. Murmurs drifted from tents. The clink of armor. A child's cry, hushed gently. The scent of boiled herbs from a healer's corner. Life was limping forward.

Then a shift.

The flap of Blu's tent opened.
Astryd stepped out.

Hopps froze.

Her silhouette caught the morning light, gold bleeding around her like a halo that didn't belong. Her hair was loose, cascading down her back in tangled waves. No armor. No sword. No mask. She looked... soft. Not weak. Never weak. But softened in the way only grief can do. Weathered but standing.

Her eyes met his.

He felt it before he could name it. That thread. That tether between them that had frayed, nearly snapped tug tight again. Not a plea. Not a command. Just: *I'm still here.*

Hopps gave a small nod.
She returned it.

No one said a word. And yet everything was said.

A beat later, Blu emerged behind her calm, unreadable, steady. Her gaze didn't cling. She gave Astryd space. Always space. But Hopps could feel it: the gravity of her presence.
She had gone into the fire and come out unburned.

For the first time, he truly looked at her. Not as a cleric. Not as a mystery. But as the one who had reached the centre of Astryd's storm and stayed.

He didn't know what to say. How do you thank someone for saving the woman you love in ways you couldn't?

Hopps tried. He shifted. Opened his hands like he might sign something. **Thank you. I see you. I owe you everything.** But the movements never came. Instead, he just stood there, heart wide open and bleeding in silence.

Blu looked over.

And smiled.

Not warmly. Not gently. But knowingly. The kind of smile that said, **You don't have to say it. I already know.**

Later, when the makeshift war council gathered dusty maps spread on cracked tables, names recited of the dead and missing, plans whispered for what came next Astryd took her seat at the head.

She didn't sit like a queen. She sat like a survivor. A woman reborn in ash.

Blu sat beside her. Not as a second. Not as an advisor. As an anchor.

And Hopps? He stayed close. Always close. His hands signed when needed, passing information, coordinating with scouts. But his eyes never left her.
She was still burning. But now, he wasn't afraid of the fire. Because it no longer looked like it was consuming her.

That night, as the sky bled into deep violet and stars blinked overhead, Hopps found her again.

She was sitting by the fire. Alone this time. Watching the flames. He sat beside her. Not touching. Not pushing. Just *present*. Astryd leaned into him, her shoulder brushing his. Her head tilted, resting just enough that he could feel her breath against his collar.

Her fingers reached for his. Not tight. Not desperate. Just… seeking. He took her hand. No words passed between them. They didn't need them.

She was still here. He was still hers. And for one fragile, fleeting night that was enough.

Far from camp, the cold crept deeper into the bones of the earth. Beneath the surface, something shifted. Something ancient. Something hungry. Because death, once tasted, always leaves a trail.

And this story this war, this love,

this reckoning was far from over.

Chapter thirty nine: A Promise in the Ashes

The night crept in slowly, curling around the camp like a second skin. Fires burned low, casting long shadows that flickered like ghosts across the broken ground. Guards rotated with hushed footsteps, their eyes wary. The wounded shifted in uneasy sleep, some whispering in dreams, others caught in silence too heavy to break. But Astryd stayed awake.

She sat on a stone half-buried in blackened earth, her cloak pulled tightly around her shoulders, eyes fixed on the sky. The stars blinked down without mercy cold, uncaring. Distant reminders that the world went on, even when you didn't.

The air smelled of ash and blood and spent magic, but none of it touched her. She felt outside of it all, her breath shallow in her chest, her heartbeat a drum lost in fog.

Blu's presence still lingered in her memory like the echo of a song she couldn't unhear. Not because of the words spoken, but because of the silence that had held her together. And Hopps… Hopps was something else entirely. A steady pull in her chest. The gravity that never demanded, only offered.

She didn't know how to feel. She only knew that something had shifted. The armor she always wore not the forged metal kind, but the armor of will, of pride, of control felt cracked. Not shattered, but changed. And beneath those cracks, something living stirred again. Fragile. Furious. Real.

Hopps moved beside her, quiet as always. He didn't disturb the moment, didn't break it with sound or question. He was just there.

She didn't startle. She'd known he would come. Knew he'd wait until she was ready to be seen again not by the camp, not by the council, but by him.

He didn't sit immediately. He stood a few feet away, his breath visible in the cold night air, watching her profile. Watching the way the wind played with strands of her hair. The way the firelight kissed her cheekbones. And then, slowly, he knelt beside her.

Astryd turned to him, her expression unguarded for the first time in what felt like years. Her eyes were softer than they'd been in weeks, though they still shimmered with the weight of what she carried.

"*I'm sorry*," she said, voice raw. Not forced. Just true.

Hopps didn't move. Didn't breathe. Just waited.

"*I've carried too much,*" she went on, her fingers twitching at her sides. "*And I let it twist me. I let it turn everything into fire and fury. And I kept thinking... if I burned bright enough, maybe I wouldn't have to feel the grief.*"

She reached out then, brushing a finger over his gloved hand.

"*But it's still here. It always will be.*"

He nodded slowly. Then raised his hands.

I never asked you to stop burning, he signed, hands steady in the low light.

Astryd let out a breath that trembled. Her chest ached with it.

Hopps continued. *I just wanted to burn with you. Not outside the flame. Beside it.*

Astryd blinked fast. She had been so afraid terrified that if she ever let go, really let go, she'd lose herself completely. That she'd become nothing but the fire and forget who she was beneath it.

But Blu hadn't tried to pull her back. She had simply stayed. Held the space. And Hopps Hopps had stood at the edge, waiting. Not turning away. Not demanding. Just… present.

Astryd leaned into him now, their foreheads gently touching, the connection grounding her more than any spell ever could.

"*I don't know how to be that person again,*" she whispered. "*The one from before.*"

Hopps signed slowly. *Then don't be. Be the one who survived.*

Her eyes glistened, but no tears fell. Not now. Not with him. The breaking had already happened. What came next wasn't collapse. It was reclamation.

Without a word, Hopps reached into his pack and pulled something out a small satchel wrapped in faded red cloth, worn soft with time. He opened it carefully, reverently, and set it between them.

Inside were three items. A dried flower, pressed flat and delicate. A broken compass, its needle spinning with no destination. And a charm shaped like a flame.

Astryd's breath hitched.

"From the temple?" she asked.

He nodded.

"I thought you lost these."

He signed, *I didn't want to remember then.*
But now? These are all I have left of the day I first knew I loved you.

The confession landed soft and heavy, like snowfall over scorched earth.

It didn't need a grand moment. It didn't need a speech. It was all there, in the way he laid the items before her. In the way he didn't ask her for anything in return.

Astryd traced the charm with trembling fingers.

"I should've told you sooner," she whispered. *"I love you. I think I always have."*

He smiled not wide, not triumphant. Just real. Grounded. Grateful.

"I don't want to carry this alone any more," she said, quieter than breath.

Hopps nodded. His hands settled gently over hers. *Then don't.*

The wind shifted, carrying the faint scent of woodsmoke and lavender. And with it came another presence. A step soft in the dirt. A ripple in the stillness.

Blu.

She moved like dusk fluid, certain, calming. She didn't interrupt. She didn't intrude. She simply lowered herself to the earth across from them, her gaze sweeping between the two warriors who had spent too long carrying pain like a second weapon.

Her expression held no pity. No judgment. Only kinship. Deep. Familiar.

"You don't need to prove yourselves to anyone," she said softly, voice low and even. *"You've already lived through fire. Now it's time to live through freedom."*

Astryd's spine straightened. Hopps's shoulders loosened. The tension that had wrapped itself around them for days eased by degrees.

Blu continued, *"I will stand with you both. As your shield. As your friend. As the one who remembers the truths you tried to bury."*

Her words weren't ceremonial. They weren't vows. They were something stronger.

They were a promise.

Astryd looked at her then, really looked. And something cracked open not the same kind of crack that breaks a person, but the kind that lets the light in.

"Thank you," she said. *"For seeing the parts of me I was too afraid to face."*

Blu leaned in, gently pressed her forehead to Astryd's. *"That's what sisters do."*

Hopps, silent all this time, extended his hand to brush both of their arms. His throat worked around the lump there, his voice rising in a whisper, rough and soft.

"We rise. Together."

And for the first time in what felt like forever, the ash didn't feel like an ending.

It felt like soil.

And from that soil, they would build something new. Together.

Chapter forty: What Power Demands

The relic pulsed.

Even in silence, even without magic flaring, it breathed like a living thing. Nestled in Astryd's palm, it radiated heat and hunger an echo of everything she had been, and everything she was still becoming.

She stood at the edge of the ruined clearing, boots sinking slightly into earth scorched and softened by ash. The sky above was still tinged with the bruises of dawn, streaks of violet and iron red casting long shadows through the skeletal trees. The battlefield had quieted. But within her, the storm hadn't ended it had only shifted. Changed shape. Changed voice.

Where blood had once soaked the soil, wildflowers now dared to bloom through the char, impossibly bright. Tiny blossoms of violet and gold, stubborn in their defiance. Drawn by some unseen force, as if the land itself had felt her awakening and answered.

Behind her, Blu watched with the stillness of a mountain. Her cloak, deep as the night sky, whispered faintly against the wind. Calm. Poised. Priestess and protector, sentinel and soul keeper. She did not speak, but her presence was grounding.

Hopps stood to Astryd's left, the way he always had half-shadow, half-light. His stance wasn't tense with battle-readiness. It was something else. Devotion. His fingers twitched at his sides, itching to reach out, but he didn't move. He simply watched her. Every breath she took. Every subtle shift in her posture.

The firelight caught the set of his jaw, the way his shoulder blades pulled tight beneath his cloak. And in his eyes was a question*: Are you still mine, in this power?*

Neither of them spoke it aloud.

But Astryd felt it. All of it.

The relic burned hotter in her hand.

"*I don't know if this is mine,*" she said finally, her voice barely audible beneath the rustle of wind. "*Or if it ever was.*"

Blu stepped forward, the movement graceful, deliberate. Her voice was low but unshaken. "*That's not the question. The question is what does it want from you? And what will you give it?*"

Astryd stared down at the artifact veined with gold, bone, and something darker than stone. It pulsed against her skin like a second heartbeat. It wasn't just magic. It was will. Purpose. Memory. Something ancient and wild, something that didn't simply *grant* power it demanded it. It didn't obey.

It bartered. Hopps's hands moved. Controlled, but shaking.

You've already given it something it couldn't take your life. Now it wants your soul. But it doesn't get that unless you let it.

Astryd swallowed, her throat tight.

"*I'm not sure I can tell where I end and it begins any more,*" she said. "*I feel it when I sleep. I feel it when I breathe. It wants more. It's always hungry.*"

Blu's voice turned cold and sharp, wrapped in the steel of faith. "*Then make it want you. Command it. Don't wield it like a blade. Bind with it. Show it you are sovereign.*"

Her hands trembling, Astryd stepped into the circle. Sigils had been carved deep into the ground etched in soot, blood, and will. They glowed faintly beneath her boots. Not warding. Not protection.

Focus.

She exhaled and closed her eyes. The relic lifted slightly in her grip and settled against her chest, over her heart, where it could feel every shuddering beat.

"*Show me,*" she whispered. "*What you are.*"

The reaction was instant.

Her vision darkened not with blindness, but immersion. Like she had fallen backward into black water. She didn't float. She sank.

The relic opened to her in flashes: visions of fire, of broken cities and screaming gods. Towers burning. Kingdoms crumbling. Lovers falling in pools of red. Her name howled in a hundred dying tongues.

She staggered in the circle, knees nearly giving. Breath rasping.

Hopps started forward on instinct, but Blu's hand caught his wrist.

"She has to go through it," she said softly. *"Let her drown, Hopps. That's how she'll learn to breathe in it."*

His jaw flexed. He didn't move. His gaze didn't waver.

Astryd dropped hard to one knee. The relic flared like a star in her grasp. Her skin shimmered runes etching across her arms and collarbones, lines of light and shadow stitched in divine script. Her magic. The relic's. Something else.

She held on. She *would* hold on.

In the vision, she was a thousand versions of herself. Child. Queen. Monster. Sacrifice. Warrior. Saint. She saw herself crowned in flame, drenched in blood, weeping on altars built from bone. She saw herself lost. She saw herself loved. She saw the edge of what she could become and it terrified her.

The relic didn't show her triumph. It showed her **choice.**

Kill. Command. Submit. Destroy. Transcend.

It didn't want to shape her. It wanted her to choose what kind of god she would be. She screamed and it wasn't pain. It wasn't rage. It was *defiance*. The scream didn't echo in the clearing it shattered the vision.

Her eyes flew open. And she was standing. Not on her knees any more. The relic floated just above her palm, no longer heavy, no longer searing. It waited. Not as a weapon. Not as a leash.

As a mirror.

"I understand now," she said, her voice shaking but whole. *"You don't want a master. You want a partner."*

The relic pulsed once. Deep. Low. Like the nod of something ancient that had finally *seen* her. Hopps stepped forward slowly, reverently. His hands moved with care.

What did it show you?

Astryd looked from him to Blu and back again. Her eyes didn't tremble. *"Everything I could be."*

Blu's lips curved into a soft, knowing smile. There was pride behind it. Not arrogance. Not ownership. Just pride the kind that came from watching someone stand in the wreckage of themselves and *rise*.

"And?" she asked.

Astryd lifted her chin. Her spine straightened beneath the weight of everything she now carried. *"I'm not afraid of becoming her any more."*

But even as the words left her lips, her knees buckled. Not from weakness.

From acceptance.

Hopps caught her before she hit the ground. His arms were strong, sure, and his hands held her like she was the most sacred thing he'd ever touched.

"You did it," Blu said, kneeling beside them. Her voice was low, sure. *"You faced it. And you didn't run."*

Astryd laughed, breathless. It broke from her like wind through shattered glass.

"I thought it was going to consume me."

"It still might," Blu replied. *"But now it'll do so on your terms."*

Hopps's fingers moved again. *You've turned the tide. The relic serves you now. Not the other way around.*

Astryd looked between them her partner in fire, her sister in soul and for the first time, the power inside her didn't feel like a burden.

It felt like purpose.

She rose again, slower this time, her fingers curling around the relic. Not in fear. In respect.

The sigils dimmed. The wind shifted.

The storm wasn't gone. But it *answered* to her now.

"Then let's begin," she said, voice clear, steady.

Blu stepped into the circle beside her. *"Lesson one: power listens best to those who don't speak to be heard."*

Hopps followed, never looking away.

"And to those who burn," he signed, *"not to destroy but to protect."*

And so they began.

Not just magic.

Not just legacy.

But the first true lesson of control. Of choice.

Of becoming.

Chapter forty one: The Weight of Memory

The clearing still bore scars burnt bark, scorched runes, the lingering scent of old blood soaked deep into the soil. But the air felt different now. Charged. Expectant. Not with danger, but with intent.

Astryd stood at the centre, the relic resting in her palm, pulsing in quiet rhythm. The beat no longer fought her. No longer screamed for control. It matched her own, calm and steady. Waiting.

This moment wasn't about survival any more. This was something else.

Evolution.

Hopps was already there. He stood at the southern edge of the ritual circle, quiet and still, wrapped in his cloak. The early morning dew clung to the fabric like the breath of ghosts. He didn't speak. He rarely did when others were present. But Astryd had seen the look in his eyes the tension in his jaw, the tightness around his gaze. Not fear. Not worry. Awe.

He had signed one phrase to her earlier, before the sun had risen fully over the camp: ***I'll be where you need me.***

And he was. He always was.

Blu arrived next. She stepped into the clearing like a tide washing across stone unhurried, graceful, inevitable. Her staff gleamed with soft light, silver-blue catching on the breeze, and her ceremonial robe swayed around her legs, inked with sacred runes across the hem and chest. She didn't look like a warrior today. She looked like something older. A guide. A guardian of forgotten truths.

Her gaze locked with Astryd's, and beneath the calm was something unmistakable.

Conviction.

"We begin," Blu said, her voice low and steady. ***"Not with force. Not with control. But with memory."***

Astryd's brow creased. *"**Memory?**"*

Blu stepped forward. *"**Power without memory is chaos. You have to know what the relic carries before you can wield it fully. What it remembers. What it sees in you.**"*

Astryd hesitated. Her fingers curled around the relic. The idea of facing more truths, more weight it was enough to make her feel hollow.

*"**What if I don't want to see it?**"* she asked quietly.

Hopps stepped closer. His presence wasn't loud, but it was grounding. He touched her hand lightly. Not to take the relic. Just to remind her he was there.

Then, with slow, deliberate movement, he signed: ***You face it anyway. And I'll stand with you.***

Astryd gave a single nod. It wasn't much, but it was enough.

Blu knelt and drew a wide circle around them using a vial of chalk mixed with ash and oil. She whispered in Draconic, her voice wrapping around them like smoke. The runes ignited with a low, glowing flame, marking the boundary between ordinary space and sacred ground.

The wind stilled. Even the birds held their breath.

The relic flared.

Astryd didn't move, but the world shifted around her. The light folded inward. Time slipped sideways. She wasn't standing in the clearing any more.

She stood on a battlefield that didn't belong to her but felt like it had always been hers. Towers, high and twisted, burned across the horizon. Smoke curled into a sky as black as obsidian. The ground was shattered glass and ash. And everywhere she looked, she saw herself.

Reflected in the ruins. In the broken glass. In the twisted remnants of magic.

But never the same.

A tyrant. A goddess. A monster. A child. A queen.

Each reflection showed her a path what she could become, what she might already be.

Hopps's voice rang out inside her mind. Not in sound, but in memory. Not the silence she knew, but a whisper of the voice she sometimes imagined.

You are not what they fear you'll become. You are what you choose.

She stumbled, gasping for breath, but before she could fall, another figure emerged through the vision.

Blu.

She glowed with quiet power, her form steady, her eyes alight with something ancient.

"Remember who you are," she said. *"Not just the rage. Not just the pain. You. Before all of this."*

The battlefield trembled. And new images came.

Astryd as a child, scraped knees and messy braids, swinging a wooden sword too heavy for her arms. Astryd, eyes wide with wonder, lightning sparking from her fingertips by accident, her laugh breathless and terrified.

Astryd, beside Blu, laughing in a shallow river. The water up to their ankles. Sunlight in her hair.

Astryd, reaching for Hopps's hand not in desire, not in battle, but in trust.

The memory hit harder than anything else. The vision cracked apart like glass under pressure. Then everything stilled. And she was back.

The clearing rushed in around her. Her knees hit the earth. Her chest rose and fell, fast and shaky. But she didn't let go of the relic. It floated above her hand, burning low, like an ember waiting for breath.

Hopps knelt beside her, his hands moving quickly, urgently. *What did you see?*

She looked at them both. Her voice came out raw, but her eyes were steady.

"I remembered. Everything. Everything I buried. Everything I broke. And everything worth saving."

Blu lowered herself into a crouch, staff grounding into the dirt beside her.

"That's the second lesson," she said gently. *"To wield power without losing the pieces of yourself that once knew how to love."*

Hopps reached for her other hand, and this time, she didn't pull away. There was no need.

"I thought strength meant letting it all go," Astryd whispered. *"I thought if I carried any of it, it would destroy me."*

Blu shook her head slowly. *"Strength is carrying it anyway. Even when it shakes you. Even when it breaks you. Especially then."*

"You are the blade," Blu said, *"but also the hand that chooses not to swing it. That's what makes you worthy."*

Astryd gave a small smile. Not wide. Not bright. But real. And for now, that was enough.

The relic's light dimmed still warm, still alive, but no longer resisting. It had seen her. And now, it would follow.

She rose slowly, Hopps's hand in hers, Blu on her other side.

Not student and teacher any more. Not protector and wielder.

Something new.

A bond forged through fire, held steady by faith, and now grounded in will.

They stood together in the stillness. And as the sun broke over the treetops, painting the clearing in gold and smoke, it didn't feel like the aftermath of war any more.

It felt like the beginning of something greater.

Chapter forty two: What Remains Must Rise

They found the village at dawn.

The smoke was thin now no longer the black plumes of active ruin but a pale grey haze that clung to the bones of houses like ghosts reluctant to leave.

What hadn't been burned had been broken. Doors dangled from rusted hinges. Stone walls were cratered and cracked, scarred by explosions of magic and force. The silence of morning didn't bring peace. It was heavy. Unnatural. More oppressive than a battlefield scream.

Astryd stood at the front of the group, her cloak pulling in the wind, trailing against her boots as if even the fabric could sense the grief waiting ahead. The relic pressed against her chest beneath her armor, strangely quiet, like even it understood the difference between vengeance and this this sorrow.

Behind her, Hopps and Blu waited in steady silence. No commands were needed. No words. They moved like a unit now three souls orbiting the same grief-wounded sun. Further back, others emerged: scouts with dirt on their cheeks, healers shouldering too many losses, mages too young to know that sometimes magic couldn't fix everything.

They'd come because of a message. No fanfare. Just a desperate scrawl on parchment, carried by blistered hands: *A village razed. Survivors barely breathing. Something hunts in the woods.*

There would be no glory here. No speeches. No banners.
Just **need**. And need was harder to face than bloodshed.

Astryd shifted her weight slightly, boots crunching in the soot. Her hands, still bandaged from the last surge of power, twitched with phantom fire. She could smell the ruin already ash, rot, the sour sting of old blood and older magic.

She drew in a breath. It didn't help. She wasn't afraid. But she was uncertain.

Who was she now? Not the girl who had fallen. Not the flame that had risen from the dead. Not merely the commander or the wielder of the relic.

What did a village need from someone like her?

Could she **give** what they needed without destroying more than she saved?

Her steps faltered. Barely. But Hopps noticed. Of course he noticed.

He didn't move. Didn't reach for her. But his presence shifted an invisible thread drawn tighter. Like a hand at the small of her back. Reassurance, not correction. Support, not control.

And beside him, Blu stood with her arms crossed. Her face gave nothing away, but her presence was like stone beneath Astryd's feet. A silent reminder that she didn't have to walk into this alone.

Astryd exhaled. The breath felt heavier than armor. Then she stepped forward.

The village welcomed them with the kind of silence that didn't feel empty it felt haunted.

Up close, it was worse.

Chairs blackened to splinters. Cribs overturned. Blood soaked into cracked wood like it had been trying to vanish, to bury the evidence of loss. Furniture lay in piles in the square like pyres that never caught flame. Collapsed beams blocked doorways. A child's toy lay abandoned in a puddle of soot.

And in the centre of it all, a woman knelt beside a broken fountain. Her hands were stained red. Not her blood. Her eyes locked onto Astryd the moment she arrived sunken, hollow, but blazing with something deeper than hope.

"You came," the woman said.

Not a thank you. Not a challenge. Just a truth. A statement in the voice of someone who had no breath left for anything else.

Astryd opened her mouth. No words came. No orders. No speeches. Just silence.

And then, she knelt. She didn't posture. Didn't raise her head like a commander. She lowered herself to the woman's eye level.

"What do you need?" she asked.

And the woman wept. They went to work.

Astryd didn't issue commands for vengeance. There were no cries for justice, no drawn swords. She walked through the ruins. She listened. She helped carry bodies. She healed where she could and where she couldn't, she simply stood beside those who could.

She did not summon the storm. She did not draw on the relic. She offered presence instead of power. Mercy instead of flame.

Hopps moved with her like a shadow woven from steel always one step behind, always watching. His hands signed gently to a boy who hadn't spoken in days. The boy nodded once. Just once. But it was enough. A crack in the fear. The beginning of trust.

Blu worked in silence, too. Casting barriers to reinforce what buildings remained, whispering blessings over those huddled in corners of wreckage. Her fingers traced sigils into dirt. Her eyes never missed a soul.

Across the square, her gaze met Astryd's once. And she smiled not with pride, not with sympathy, but with solidarity.

By the time the sun began to fall, when the sky turned to amber and the shadows grew long, the worst had been done.

The bodies were laid out. The fires were out. The wounded had been fed, bandaged, seen.

Astryd slumped against a half-burned fence at the edge of the village. Her shoulders ached from lifting debris. Her knees bore the grime of too many prayers spoken through action. The relic at her chest pulsed faintly, as if offering comfort or acknowledgment.

Hopps dropped beside her, careful not to disturb her quiet. He didn't speak. He never did when the moment didn't ask for it.

But after a pause, his hands moved. ***You didn't burn.***

Astryd turned her head to look at him. Her expression was tired, but steady.

"I wanted to," she admitted.

His fingers moved again. ***But you didn't.***

Her fingers drifted to the relic, and she nodded. *"Because I remembered."*

Remembered what? he signed.

"Who I wanted to be."

He reached for her hand. She let him take it. They sat like that as the sky darkened. No speeches. No declarations. Just hands joined beneath a sky that had seen too much.

Blu joined them not long after. She lowered herself slowly, her legs stiff from kneeling too long beside the injured. She didn't say anything at first.

She didn't have to.

Astryd leaned her head back against the fence. Hopps leaned his shoulder into hers.

And Blu watched them both like someone watching something ancient and sacred renew itself. No flames. No relics. Just the three of them breathing in the stillness of what had been saved.

The village slept.

No banners flew. No horns sounded.

But something had been rebuilt here.

What remained had survived.

And from it, something new would rise.

Chapter forty three: The Flame and the Vow

The return from the village was quiet.

Not silent, not hollow, but the kind of quiet that only follows survival. The kind that lets you breathe again. That strange stillness after screaming stops and wounds begin to close. The air carried the scent of wet earth and mended wounds, of smoldering grief being slowly buried beneath rebuilding hands. Homes were rising. Slowly. Unevenly. But rising.

The sky, painted in violet dusk, mirrored the ash-and-gold that clung to Astryd's shoulders as she led them back toward camp. Her steps were steady now, but her gaze drifted far like she walked not on soil but on memory.

The villagers had bowed to her. Had thanked her. Had whispered her name like it meant something sacred. Not in fear. In *hope*.

And that? That terrified her more than their screams ever had.

She walked alone for a while. The path wound between scorched trees and new growth, the borderlands between what had been ruined and what might rise again. Behind her, Blu followed with soft steps, offering silence and space the way only a true soul-sister could. Hopps was never far just a few paces back, always watching. A steady shadow. A silent vow.

Neither rushed her. Neither called her name. They understood, now more than ever, that sometimes quiet was the only sanctuary you could offer someone who had been broken open and stitched back together with fire.

At the edge of a stream, Astryd stopped.

The water shimmered beneath the dying light, reflecting the first stars blooming in the indigo sky. She crouched, letting her fingers drift over the surface. The ripples that danced outward echoed everything still moving inside her grief, restraint, the ache of held-back power. She had stood in the ruins of that village and *not burned*. That choice had cost her something.

But it had given her something, too.

Hopps moved first.

He didn't speak. He didn't need to.

She felt him before she saw him, his presence folding into the space beside her like a breath she hadn't realized she was holding. When she turned to him, her eyes locked onto his, and he froze, not because of heat, but because there wasn't any.

The fire in her wasn't gone. It was contained.

"I could've burned them all," she said softly, the confession like embers falling from her lips. *"And a part of me wanted to. To make the pain simple. Clean."*

Hopps didn't flinch. He just signed: ***But you didn't.***

She nodded once. *"No. I chose to see what could be rebuilt instead of what could be destroyed."*

Her voice cracked around the edges. Her fingers drifted to the relic resting against her chest. It pulsed slow. Soft. Like it had finally yielded. Not out of fear. Not out of conquest. But *grace*.

Blu approached then, stepping through the soft underbrush like dusk itself. Her presence wrapped around them both not smothering, but steadying. She didn't interrupt. Just listened until it was time to speak.

"It's never weakness to want peace," Blu said. *"Not when you've known war that deeply."*

Astryd's head bowed for a moment, as though the weight of the words landed somewhere she hadn't yet dared to look.

Then she rose.

She looked between them her two constants. Blu, her compass. Hopps, her anchor. The only ones who had seen *all* of her, and stayed.

"I don't know what comes next," Astryd said. *"I don't know what we'll face. Or what I'll have to become to survive it."* Her voice

dropped, barely more than breath. **"But I know what I need beside me."**

She reached for Hopps first. Her hand slipped into his like it belonged there not with desperation, but with choice. His eyes gleamed—not with victory, but with quiet reverence. She could feel the strength in his grip. He wasn't holding her back.

He was holding her *steady*.

Then she turned to Blu. Her other hand reached out, palm open. **"You've both walked me out of the dark more times than I can count,"** she said. **"Let me build something now that keeps the dark at bay."**

They didn't kneel. There were no rituals. No dramatic proclamations. This wasn't a coronation. It was a promise. A vow made not to gods or relics or thrones but to each other. Made in the language of scars. Of silence. Of fire tempered by love. Blu stepped forward, placing her hand over Astryd's heart. Her voice was soft, but it carried like gospel. **"Then rise,"** she said. **"Not as what they fear. But as what they never saw coming."**

Hopps raised his other hand and signed, slow and clear: *Not alone. Never again.*

The relic at Astryd's chest flared once not violently, but brilliantly. A flash of light that didn't scorch. That didn't destroy. It illuminated. It **blessed.**

And for a moment, all three stood there hands linked, hearts aligned and the air shifted. Not with magic. With *meaning*.

The stars brightened above them. The stream flowed on, carrying away the last flecks of ash from their boots, their cloaks, their wounds. Everything that had once marked ruin.

Astryd looked down at her hands. They weren't shaking. She didn't feel like a weapon anymore. She felt like a *beginning*.

She felt like fire reborn into purpose.

And in that moment, the vow wasn't just *spoken*.

It was sealed.

Chapter forty four: Old Blood, New Enemies

The stars had not yet faded when the first signs of something darker crept through the trees.

Astryd felt it first a thrum in the relic against her chest, pulsing with a warning she didn't yet understand. It beat like a second heart, urgent and insistent, stirring something ancient in her blood, something not quite her own.

The camp stirred slowly. Warriors still wrapped in sleep, mages pulling on cloaks, healers warming water for poultices and tea unaware of what moved beneath the canopy, what approached on feet wrapped in silence and intent.

It wasn't until the birds went still that Blu rose, her hand tightening around the carved hilt of her staff. Hopps, already halfway through his second perimeter check, froze mid-step. His gaze snapped to Astryd's tent, where pale light leaked from the seams. The relic's glow had changed no longer gentle, but wild. Restless.

The kind of glow that warned of blood.

Something old was coming.

The warning arrived on the back of a scout's last breath.

He stumbled into camp, torn and barely upright, eyes wide and shining with death's last glimmer. His body shook as he dropped to one knee, hands clutching his side. His lips parted.

One word. Just one. **"Malrec."** The name cleaved the air like a blade.

Every movement in camp stopped. Breath caught. Fire crackled, too loud in the silence.

Astryd stood, her face drained of blood, hand already curling around the hilt of her weapon. The relic at her chest pulsed like thunder. Blu was at her side in seconds. Hopps appeared a breath later, silent but present, his eyes unreadable and locked onto hers.

Malrec.

Not dead. Not gone. And worse he *knew* about the relic. By the time the horizon cracked with dawn, the enemy stood just beyond the wards. As if he'd waited for sunrise. As if he *wanted* to be seen.

He hadn't changed.

Tall. Elegant. Unsettling. His hair was longer, bound in silver rings. His robes were deep violet, his plated armor veined with abyssal runes. A blade hung at his side, but he hadn't drawn it. He didn't need to. His smile was the weapon.

He looked like a man who had walked straight out of every nightmare Astryd had buried untouched by time, by guilt, by ruin.

"You always did underestimate me," Malrec said, voice smooth as oil.

"I didn't come here to finish what we started," he added, like this was a reunion and not the re-ignition of war.

Astryd didn't flinch. Her spine straightened.

"Then speak," she said flatly, **"*before I end it.*"**

He chuckled low, rich, like it amused him to be underestimated. **"*You could try,*"** he murmured. **"But this time, you'd be wasting more than fury. You'd be wasting power you barely understand."**

The relic throbbed, the heat beneath her breastbone flaring as if in answer. Astryd didn't move, but the wind did shifting suddenly, dragging ash in little spirals across the dirt. Hopps stepped closer. His presence was no longer just silent support. It was defense. *Claim.*

Blu stood steady on her other side. Together, they made a line he could not cross.

"You want the relic," Astryd said. Not a question.

Malrec's smile widened.

"I don't want to destroy you, Astryd," he said. **"*I want to use you.*"**

His voice lowered like a lover's whisper. *"With that relic bound to your soul, you're more than a warrior. You're a conduit. A gate. You could bring entire cities to their knees without lifting a blade. Give it to me and I'll spare the next one."*

Her jaw locked. Her fingers curled, but she didn't reach for her weapon. She didn't need to. The fire beneath her skin was alive again. Ready.

"And if I don't?" she asked.

His smile never faded. *"Then their blood is on your hands. Not mine. You choose who dies."*

Silence fell, the kind that makes your ears ring.

Behind her, the camp bristled with warriors drawing blades, mages whispering incantations under their breath. Astryd didn't look back. She didn't have to. They trusted her. And she knew without question they would follow.

Hopps stood taller beside her. His hand hovered near his hilt, but his voice remained quiet, grounded, *hers*.

"You don't get to barter with monsters," he said. Not to Malrec. To *her*.

Blu took a step closer, her gaze locked on Astryd's face.

"He cannot wield what he does not understand," she said. *"But you can."*

Astryd's eyes never left Malrec. Her voice, when it came, was fire hammered into steel.

"You mistake me for someone still afraid to burn," she said.

She raised one hand, palm open. The relic flared, white-hot and sudden. The air shimmered around her, like the heat of a forge. Not a threat.

A truth. *"You think this relic binds me. But it answers me."*

The flame danced, not from the relic but from her. Controlled. Contained. Willing.

"You want power?" she whispered. *"Go find your own."*

Then lower, sharper. A blade in words. *"But if you come near my people again, you won't just lose a city."*

She stepped forward. *"You'll lose yourself."*

And for the first time in years, Malrec's smile *faltered*. Just slightly. But it was enough.

The trees groaned with the weight of their tension. A hawk screamed somewhere high above. Beneath the earth, something ancient stirred.

"Then you've made your choice," he said coldly. *"Let's hope the world survives it."*

He turned, cloak swirling behind him, and vanished into the woods. The shadows swallowed him without a sound. Astryd stood still long after he was gone. Her breath was slow. Measured.

Hopps stood beside her. Watching. Waiting. Blu placed a hand on her shoulder not guiding her. Grounding her. She didn't tremble.

But when she turned to face them, her eyes weren't just fire anymore. They were *purpose*.

"We ride at dawn," she said. *"If he wants war, he'll learn what it means to fight someone who's already died and come back stronger."*

The war hadn't ended.

It had only evolved.

And Astryd was no longer playing by the rules.

She was *rewriting* them.

In fire. In blood. In light.

FLASHBACK: The Fall of Valebright

Valebright had been a city of light.

Towers of gold and glass. Laughter in the halls of magic. Incantations that sang through the streets. A place where power was studied not feared. Where magic was art. Where Astryd had **belonged.**

And Malrec? He had walked those streets like a prophet.

A teacher. A guide. He had taken her under his wing, told her she was chosen. He taught her to feel power in silence, to bend light to her will. Whispered secrets of the old gods. Gave her scrolls that trembled with forgotten knowledge.

"You have the kind of soul," he'd said, *"that calls to both the divine and the abyss."*

And she had believed him. Until the day her mother screamed. Until the sky tore open. Until the sanctum walls melted into flame and stone. Until her hands were red with the blood of those she couldn't save.

The library had burned first. With the children still reading inside. Their voices quiet, trusting had been the last she heard before the fire swallowed everything. Then the sanctum. Then the high tower where she had promised to return before nightfall.

And through it all, Malrec had smiled.

"You are the spark," he'd whispered as the city burned. *"Now become the flame."*

She had fled. Smoke in her lungs. Ash in her mouth. Grief dragging at her heels like chains.

She carried that name **Valebright** not with pride.

But with sorrow. A scar that never closed.

And now, as she watched him walk again from the trees like he hadn't torn the world apart, Astryd felt something rise within her that wasn't fear.

It was fire.

Pure.

Unyielding.

Because she wasn't the girl who had run from the ruin.

She *was* the ruin.

And Malrec had no idea what he'd just reignited.

Chapter forty five: Rising Flame

The echo of Malrec's name still lingered long after he vanished into the woods like a toxin in the air. It didn't just rattle the warriors standing in defense.

It reached deeper. Into memory. Into fear. Into the tethered line between past and power.

The camp didn't sleep that night. Not truly. Not fully. There were no dreams. Just the steady rhythm of preparation. Weapons were cleaned with a reverence that bordered on ritual. Armour was checked and re-checked until buckles creaked and fingers bled. Magic circles were re-drawn into the dirt, symbols pressed harder than needed just to feel control over *something*.

They weren't preparing for war. They were preparing for *him*.

At the edge of the ward line, Astryd stood alone. Motionless. The wind brushed her cloak like fingers too afraid to touch. The relic at her chest pulsed not violently, not wildly, but with a steady, hungry rhythm. Like a beast that had tasted blood and was waiting for the next command.

It beat in time with her. A second heart. A deeper breath beneath her own. She didn't blink as the stars wheeled overhead. Didn't flinch when the wind changed.

She felt it before anyone else. It started in her fingertips. A warmth. A pressure. A whisper. The relic wasn't warning her**. It was *calling* her.**

Blu stepped beside her like the night had conjured her. A shadow turned flesh. No words at first. Just presence. Just *gravity*.

"You haven't let yourself feel it yet," Blu said, voice low, eyes fixed on the black horizon.

Astryd's throat worked. *"If I let it in... I don't know what I'll become."*

Blu's response was gentle, but unflinching. ***"Then become her. But do it on your terms."***

Behind them, Hopps appeared without sound, his footsteps swallowed by the earth. He didn't speak he never did unless it was for her. But she felt him like gravity. Like home.

When she turned to him, he was already watching. ***Do you trust it?*** he signed.

Her hand hovered over the relic. *"I don't know yet,"* she whispered.

He stepped closer, reaching out. His fingers settled over her chest, just above the relic. Calloused and warm. A grounding weight. A promise. ***Then trust yourself first.***

It was always like that with Hopps. Fewer words. Deeper meaning. His voice only ever belonged to *her*.

Astryd turned back toward the forest. The path Malrec had vanished down hours earlier was still and quiet but it buzzed beneath the surface. The night held its breath.

"He thinks I'm still the girl who burned," she murmured.

Blu didn't hesitate. ***"You are the girl who burned. But you're also the woman who walked back through the ashes."***

The relic sparked at that. Just once. A flare against her collarbone. Astryd flinched, but didn't look away.

"I want to understand it," she said. *"I need to. Before he uses it me against everything we've built."*

Blu nodded. ***"Then we begin at dawn. But not as a lesson."*** She paused. ***"As a reckoning."***

Hopps stepped forward, brushing a strand of hair away from Astryd's face. His fingers lingered at her cheek not as a lover's touch, but something older. Deeper. A vow carved from battle and blood and belief.

You lead, he signed. ***We follow. Always.***

Astryd looked at them both. Blu, divine and unwavering. Hopps, silent and fierce. They were hers. Not by conquest. By *choice*. She had bled for this world. She had died for it.

But now... she would *rise* for it. And she would not rise alone. Back in her tent, sleep didn't come. She didn't expect it to.

The relic pulsed beside her, not like a weapon, but like a companion. A fire curled into her ribs. Familiar now. No longer a stranger.

She dreamt.

Of Valebright.
Of children running through glowing corridors.
Of laughter before the screams.
Of Malrec's hand on her shoulder as the sky turned to flame.

She dreamt of what she could become.

Not a queen.

Not a weapon.

But a *force*.

A goddess of her own making.

She woke before the sun rose.

Her fingers moved with practiced ease, wrapping leather straps around her arms, sliding armor over her chest armor laced with *memory*. Every buckle fastened with breath. Every layer like a new skin. She stepped outside and the cold morning met her like an old rival.

Blu and Hopps were already waiting. No words. Just readiness. Just *faith*. Astryd didn't hesitate. She walked into the dawn, the relic glowing with her heartbeat, each step solid. Grounded. Certain. She didn't look back.

"***Show me,***" she whispered.

Not to Blu. Not to Hopps. Not even to the relic. To *herself*. Because the war wasn't coming. It had *already begun*. And she was the one who would write its ending.

With fire. With freedom. And with the kind of love that never asks permission to burn.

Chapter forty six: The Weight of Vows

The air still crackled with the remnants of Malrec's threat, his name like ash that refused to settle. Tension clung to the camp in the way smoke does after fire: invisible, persistent, invasive. Dawn had broken across the horizon, but the light it brought wasn't comfort. It was a warning. A breath held too long.

Astryd hadn't slept.

She stood alone at the edge of the warding circle, where the trees met open sky. Her gaze stayed locked on the trail that snaked into the blackened woods, as if it might shift or spit him out at any moment. Her armor caught the rising light, the plates dulled from battle, the edges lined with ash that no amount of polishing could scrub away. The relic at her chest was warm not pulsing with urgency like before, but holding its own breath. Waiting. Anticipating.

As if it already knew what she would do next.

Hopps watched her from the shadows beyond the central tent, crouched between two stones half-buried in frostbitten earth. He didn't approach. Not yet. Not until she invited him. He had learned the rhythm of her silences, had learned when to give her solitude and when to shatter it. Sometimes her quiet was sacred. Sometimes it was war.

He would know the difference. Blu was the one who moved first.

She stepped from the healer's tents, her cloak rippling like water over stone. Her stride was soft but sure, and she crossed the distance without asking permission. She never needed to. She came not as a commander or priestess, but as something rarer a soul who understood what it meant to carry fire in the marrow.

"She's still watching," Blu said softly, her voice low enough not to disturb the frost. *"Whatever power stirs in the woods... it's testing your resolve."*

Astryd's eyes didn't leave the tree line. *"He's not gone."*

"*No*," Blu agreed. "Just patient. *He's seen the storm you can become. He's waiting to see if you'll turn it inward again.*"

Her voice wasn't coaxing. It wasn't pitying. It was steady. Like stone. Like truth.

Astryd's fingers brushed the relic beneath her armor. The warmth of it had become part of her more familiar now than fear, more constant than breath. It didn't feel dangerous today.

It felt like choice.

"*Do you think I can control it?*" she asked quietly. "*Or have I just been lucky?*"

Blu turned to face her, and there was no hesitation in her answer. "*I think you already are. You just haven't forgiven yourself for how long it took to try.*"

Astryd flinched, just slightly. It was true. That was the hardest part. Not the fight. Not the flames. But the forgiveness.

Behind her, Hopps rose to his feet. He moved with the ease of someone who didn't need to make noise to be known. His presence settled behind her like a shadow that shielded rather than loomed. He said nothing. But the air shifted.

She turned slightly, and there he was. Watching. Anchoring her.

The vow they hadn't spoken out loud was thicker than blood.

Blu reached into the pouch at her side and drew a blade not for battle, but for vows. The ceremonial dagger gleamed in the weak light, its hilt wrapped in worn leather, its steel etched with runes of binding. Not the kind of magic that enslaved. The kind that sealed intent. That reminded a soul who it was when the world tried to make them forget.

"*It's time,*" Blu said.

"*For what?*"

"*For your vow. Not to us. Not even to the camp. To yourself.*"

Astryd hesitated as she took the blade. Her fingers trembled, but not from fear. From the *weight* of it. From everything it symbolized. Her thumb traced the ancient script along its spine—truth in a dead language that still pulsed with memory. She looked to Hopps. He didn't speak. He didn't need to. He raised one hand and signed a single word. ***Always.***

No pressure. No push. Just belief. She turned to Blu. **"Then I vow..."**

Her voice did not quake. It *settled*. **"To lead not with wrath, but with will. To fight not because I must, but because I choose to. And to wield this power only in defense of those who cannot wield it for themselves."**

She brought the blade across her palm. The cut was small. Clean. Controlled. One drop of blood fell to the earth and the ground pulsed. Magic rippled out from the circle like a heartbeat made visible. The relic on her chest flared, light seeping through her armor like the glow of dawn beneath storm clouds. But it did not consume her.

It echoed her.

Blu stepped forward and wrapped her hand with a cloth etched in clarity runes symbols meant to hold oaths in place when the heart tried to break them. The fabric shimmered faintly as it soaked up the blood and sealed the promise in light.

"So it is written," Blu said, voice reverent. **"So it begins."**

The wind shifted.

The camp began to stir warriors stepping from tents, mages blinking sleep from their eyes. Not drawn by noise, but by *something else*. A ripple in the magic. A change in the air. An echo of flame.

They watched from the edges of the clearing.

They said nothing.

But they *felt* it.

Astryd stood taller. And Hopps stepped beside her. His hands moved again. This time slower. Firmer. A gesture practiced a thousand times. **Mine.**

She smiled. Not wide. Not loud. But true.

"Always," she said.

Blu moved to their other side, planting her staff into the earth. Light rippled outward, barely visible in the cold air. "And we rise together."

The sun crested the tree line.

Light filtered through ash and smoke, brushing over scorched earth, lighting up sparks in the firepit from the night before. The embers rose slowly tiny stars given breath and drifted into the sky.

This wasn't just a vow.

This was ignition.

Astryd had chosen her flame.

And she would no longer carry it alone.

They would not just endure what came next.

They would ignite it.

And the world?

The world would burn back to life.

Chapter forty seven: The Ember Throne

The morning after the vow felt different.

The sky seemed sharper, as though even the clouds held their breath. There was clarity in the air a hush not born of fear, but of focus. Every blade of grass stood a little taller, every breeze moved with purpose, as if the land itself knew something had shifted.

The camp was awake, but quieter than usual. Not subdued attentive. Watchful.

Astryd stepped from her tent with slow, purposeful grace. Her movements were precise, her gaze unwavering. There was no hesitation in her stride, no question in her bearing.

The relic rested against her sternum like it had always belonged there not thrumming wildly anymore, not whispering madness or burning with chaos. It pulsed now like a companion. Like breath. Like certainty.

She wasn't struggling to carry its weight.

She was becoming it.

At the edge of the camp, near the eastern clearing, Blu waited. The sacred rings had been cleared at dawn old ground, rarely used, ritually significant. Once, they had been reserved for rites of passage, for clarity and rebirth. Today, they were something more. A threshold.

The forest surrounded them like a cathedral silent, reverent.

Hopps was already there, posted just outside the ring. His arms were folded, weapons untouched, stance relaxed but alert. He didn't need steel for this moment. His presence was shield enough. His watchfulness said more than blades ever could.

His silence wasn't absence it was devotion.

Astryd crossed into the circle barefoot. She wanted to feel the earth cool and dewed beneath her soles, ancient and alive. She needed that grounding. She needed to know that whatever rose from within her power was still tethered to something real.

Blu lifted her hands not to cast, but to bear witness.

"This is not to master the relic," she said, voice low and resonant, carried on morning air like a spell in itself. *"This is to master yourself in its presence."*

Astryd nodded once. Her jaw was tight, but not with fear with readiness. Her muscles hummed with it. She placed her palm over the relic. It responded immediately.

Not violently. Not with hunger. But knowingly.

A spark of energy flared subtle, controlled. Like recognition. Like submission.

The power curled upward into her veins, warm and deliberate, like ink drawn into water. Her eyes flickered gold. Her breath hitched. The world narrowed.

Visions threatened. Smoke. Screams. Valebright in ruin. Her hands red.

But Blu was there, stepping forward, placing a steady hand on her shoulder. Her presence was an anchor. *"Anchor to now."*

Hopps moved in silence. His fingertips brushed the back of her hand a quiet reassurance. A thread of shared memory.

Astryd drew in a breath.

The visions fractured. The smoke cleared. The pain didn't vanish, but it softened. The power remained.

She lifted her hand, and the relic hovered with her. A strand of golden-red light unfurled from its core, weaving around her wrist like silk drawn from flame. It tested her not like a weapon, but like a wild thing wondering if it had truly been tamed.

Blu stepped back and began to chant not a spell of control, but one of space-clearing. The words were ancient, the cadence steady. It vibrated through the ground, subtle but potent.

The air within the circle shimmered.

Astryd took a step. The light followed. Another. Still, no fire scorched the grass. No trees curled in fear. The earth beneath her warmed not in threat, but in welcome.

"It bends to you," Blu said softly, awed. ***"Not from fear. From recognition."***

Astryd tried to speak, but no words came. Instead, her power surged in a slow, radiant wave, lighting the entire clearing in a soft, amber glow.

It didn't burn. It bloomed.

The flames sparked wildflowers in her wake golden-tipped petals pushing up through soil that once only knew ash.

From fire, life.

Hopps's expression barely shifted, but his eyes shone with something sacred. He didn't sign. He didn't speak. This moment needed neither.

Astryd lowered her hand. The relic quieted. She turned to Blu. ***"I can feel it now. Not like a storm waiting to break… like a hearth that burns for the ones I choose to keep warm."***

Blu nodded, her own voice thick with reverence. ***"Then your throne is not made of ash it is made of ember. It will burn, not to destroy, but to illuminate."***

Astryd stepped from the ring, and for the first time, the forest didn't whisper behind her. It bowed.

Hopps met her just beyond the edge, catching her wrist with one hand. He brought it to his lips not in ritual. In reverence.

Not to claim her. To honour her. She touched his jaw. Her eyes gleamed gold in the firelight.

"Then let the world come," she whispered. ***"This time, we rise together."***

The wind stirred through the trees. And as if summoned by her vow, the forest exhaled not in fear.

But in anticipation.

Chapter forty eight: Ashes Know Her Name

The wind carried word faster than any raven.

By midday, scouts returned with wide eyes and trembling hands. A neighbouring clan one long known for raiding the southern edges of the realm was approaching. Not with banners of war, but cloaked in the thin veneer of diplomacy. They called it a diplomatic visit.

But everyone knew what it was. A challenge. A test of power, of presence, of resolve.

Astryd stood at the head of the path before the camp, her silhouette sharp against the afternoon sun. She wore no armor. No crown. Only the quiet, controlled fire of someone who had nothing left to prove and yet, everything left to protect.

She was barefoot on the soil. Cloaked in the same layered blacks and ember tones she'd worn since the vow, the relic glowing faintly where it rested against her chest. Its pulse was steady. Alive. Not flaring with fury but burning with truth.

Blu stood to her right, wrapped in ceremonial white robes trimmed in ancient blue runes, each one inked by hand with sacred memory. She looked like she belonged in a temple, not on a battlefield and yet, the divine weight she carried was heavier than any sword. Her presence was not just cleric or counsellor. Today, she was reckoning made flesh.

Hopps stood on Astryd's left, tall and unreadable, a wall of calm shadow. His hands were empty. His weapons untouched. But his posture was enough. Every line of his body said: **Step wrong, and it ends here.**

He didn't speak. Not to them. Only his eyes spoke burning, unwavering, fixed solely on Astryd.

The emissary from the clan stepped forward. An ageing warrior with a voice like gravel and furs that reeked of smoke. His eyes flicked between Astryd, Blu, and Hopps with thinly veiled caution.

He held himself like a man trained to command. But his footing trembled under the weight of what stood before him.

"The fire that took Valebright has returned," he said. His words were meant to provoke but they cracked with unease. *"**You wield something none of us understand. And that makes you dangerous.**"*

Astryd didn't flinch.

Her voice, when it came, was level as iron laid in flame. *"**Only to those who would harm what I protect.**"*

The wind stirred around them. The relic responded with a soft, pulsing glow, casting light up her throat and across her jaw like holy fire. It didn't burn. It warned.

*"**You would risk war again?**"* the emissary asked, voice tightening. *"**You think that throne of ash will hold against the storms to come?**"*

She stepped forward.

The earth beneath her feet warmed and bloomed not with flame, but with golden roots and small flowers, summoned not by magic but by the *choice* to walk in power. She didn't glow. **She commanded.**

*"**My throne is not of ash,**"* she said. *"**It is ember. It does not crumble. It remembers. And it burns only when I say it should.**"*

The gathered crowd a mix of her people, her soldiers, and the visiting warriors—held their collective breath. A hundred eyes. A thousand held thoughts.

Blu lifted her chin, tilting her head to the sky. Her voice rose in a single, resonant chord a protective rite that shimmered through the clearing. It echoed like an ancient bell, stirring the leaves, thickening the air. The sound didn't threaten.

It warned. Behind her, Hopps raised one hand. Just a single gesture. And yet it drew every eye. Not a threat. A promise.

The emissary faltered. He tried to hide it, but it was there the way his jaw tensed, the way his feet shifted. The unity in front of him, the silence, the control it unsettled him more than a thousand screaming men ever could.

"You would lead them all?" he asked. *"You would claim the title left behind by blood and ruin?"*

Astryd's reply was quiet. But it cracked through the tension like thunder. *"I don't claim,"* she said. *"I inherit. And I rise not because I want to rule. I rise because someone must."*

Her hand lifted, fingers curled lightly toward her collarbone. The relic flared. Not violently. Not chaotically.

But with the slow, undeniable radiance of something ancient and awake.

And in its glow, the trees leaned closer. The ground shifted. The earth **remembered her name.**

Blu stepped forward, her voice clear and unwavering. *"Astryd of Valebright,"* she declared, *"Bearer of the Ember Relic. Keeper of the flame that survived ruin. Chosen not by blood, but by will."*

Hopps moved behind Astryd, placing one hand lightly on her back. The only touch she needed. Not control. Not guidance.

Grounding.

Strength.

The emissary swallowed. Sweat beaded at his brow. *"And if we refuse allegiance?"* he asked.

Astryd tilted her head. The fire in her eyes didn't burn. It judged. *"Then you'll find the world has already shifted beneath your feet,"* she said. *"I am not asking you to follow. I am giving you one chance not to be left behind."*

There was no surge of magic. No flare of light.

But the air shimmered like heat off stone. The earth waited.

And the emissary bowed. Not low. But enough.

"Then may the flames guide us," he said.

With that, the visitors turned and left.

Not as conquerors.

Not as equals.

But as those who finally understood: **ashes know her name now.**

As the sun dipped lower behind the trees, casting gold along the tips of the grass, Astryd turned to her companions. Blu's eyes shone with quiet pride. Hopps's hand slid into hers.

"You didn't just stand," Blu said softly. *"You shaped them."*

Astryd exhaled, slow and full. *"I'm not done yet,"* she replied.

And far to the west, from beyond the distant mountains, a column of smoke rose into the sky curling upward like a herald.

Of something coming.

Of something old.

Of something only *she* could meet.

Chapter forty nine : To War, We Rise

The forest no longer whispered. It roared low, steady, and ancient, like it too had taken the vow.

Astryd stood before the council ring. Her cloak caught in the cold wind that swept down from the northern ridges, the same wind that carried whispers of war and the scent of turned soil. The relic pulsed steadily at her chest not in alarm, but in agreement. Its heartbeat matched her own.

Around her, commanders assembled. Old veterans with tired eyes and fresh scars. Young fighters with sharpened blades and faces etched with resolve. Seers stood behind them, quiet and unreadable, their hands marked with ritual paint, their silence louder than any prophecy.

They didn't come to question her. They came to follow her. Because they had seen her fall. They had seen her burn. And still, she rose.

Hopps stood at her right, arms crossed, shoulders squared. He said nothing. He rarely did, not in public. But the way he watched the gathered warriors, the way he stood just slightly in front of her shoulder, spoke volumes. His silence was protection. His presence was an oath.

Blu stood at Astryd's left, her staff grounded beside her feet. Silver thread glinted in the blue of her robes, catching what little sunlight managed to pierce the trees. She said nothing at first. She didn't need to. Her gaze was steady, and her stillness was not passive it was reverent.

"We move at dusk," Astryd said, her voice cutting through the morning with quiet certainty. *"Three paths through the valley. Two of them shadowed by the cliffs we'll use those for misdirection. The main force rides with me through the broken pass."*

The sound that followed was not applause or cheering it was a ripple of movement. Heads nodded. Fingers flexed around hilts. Eyes sharpened. They understood. They were ready.

One voice, though, rose from the edge of the circle.

A younger warrior stepped forward. A half-elf girl, barely out of her second decade, ash-smudged and bold in her uncertainty. *"Why you?"* she asked, not with malice, but something that bordered on desperation. *"Why not the scouts? Why not command from the ridge like the last generals?"*

Astryd didn't bristle. She didn't posture. She simply stepped forward. *"Because if I ask you to face death,"* she said, calm and clear, *"you deserve to see the one who already has. And chose to return."*

The girl stared at her for a long moment, searching for something. Then she nodded. Not out of fear. Out of belief.

Astryd turned back to the stone altar. The map laid across it was rough but clear. Markers carved from bone and ash showed Malrec's movement through the valley. Already, his soldiers had begun torching outer farms. Already, refugees had started appearing in the woods, driven from their homes by a man who wanted obedience, not survival.

"This isn't just about tactics," Blu said quietly beside her. *"It's about what we leave behind when they pass through our ashes. Fear or fire."*

Astryd nodded once. *"Then we give them fire."*

Preparations followed quickly. Every movement in the camp became deliberate. Hopps slipped between the ranks, inspecting blades, redrawing protective circles, signing quick instructions to squad leaders. His silence did not slow the work it commanded it. And though he only ever spoke to Astryd, every soldier in that ring moved when he passed.

Blu worked in the grove, her hands weaving magic into the roots of the trees and the wards around the tents. She did not pray with desperation. She prayed with resolve, her spells carrying the promise of protection, not the hope for mercy.

Astryd stood on the ridge as twilight bled into the horizon, casting everything in a shade of crimson that felt prophetic. From her position, she could see the three paths clearly. In the distance, smoke coiled into the sky where farms once stood.

Her fingers brushed the relic at her chest.

She remembered. Valebright. The corridors filled with laughter. Her father's steady hands. Her mother's voice. She remembered the fire. The ash. The screams that echoed through the sanctum walls. She remembered running not in fear, but in survival.

She remembered why she was still standing.

Blu stepped up beside her. *"**This doesn't end here.**"*

"I know," Astryd said. *"**It begins.**"*

Hopps joined them without a sound. His hand found hers.

She turned toward him, rested her forehead against his for a brief moment. A tether. A grounding. *"**For them,**"* she whispered.

He signed the words back with steady fingers: *"**For you. Always.**"*

At dusk, they rode.

No banners were raised. No horns blew. Only the sound of hooves on hardened ground and the low rumble of warriors moving like a tide.

Astryd rode at the front. Her cloak rippled in the dying light. The relic gleamed like a sun caught in shadow.

Behind her, they followed not because they were ordered. Because they **believed**.

And somewhere ahead, Malrec waited.

He had spells. He had soldiers. He had cities lined up like dominos.

But he had made one fatal mistake.

He thought he was facing a woman.

He wasn't.

He was facing the storm she had become.

And this time she was not alone.

Chapter fifty: First Strike

The wind no longer whispered.
It howled.

Down the ridges and through the trees, it screamed like a herald, carrying the scent of steel and storm and the unmistakable electric sting of rising magic. This was no longer the hush before battle it was the cry that split it open.

Astryd stood at the front of the column, her cloak rippling behind her like flame catching wind. The relic hummed low against her sternum, its warmth steady and alive. It didn't pulse with uncertainty. It pulsed with purpose. No longer a beast she had to leash it was hers. Aligned. Waiting.

The land around her had grown quieter with every step, not out of fear, but respect. Even the trees seemed to lean in.

Beside her, Hopps adjusted the strap of his gear with practiced ease. His jaw was tight, his stance measured. He didn't speak. He never did when others were near. But the slight tilt of his head toward her, the near-imperceptible brush of his shoulder against hers it said everything. *I'm here. I've always been here.*

On her other side, Blu murmured the last lines of a protection ward, the edge of her voice ringing with divine tension. Her staff glowed faintly where it touched the ground, runes flaring and fading like breath.

"The wards are set," Blu said, her voice low, deliberate. **"The path to the eastern ridge is open. They won't see it coming."**

Astryd nodded. **"Good."** She didn't speak louder. She didn't have to. Every ear within range caught the word like a strike of flint. "We draw them in. Not as prey but as judgment."

Fifty fighters stood behind her, cloaked in silence and shadow. Hardened veterans, younger blades, mages whose fingers still bore the burns of learning. Their armor was dark, dulled on purpose, etched with sigils drawn in ash and blood. They weren't a war party. They were a promise.

Scouts had confirmed Malrec's movements: a probing force sent toward the high pass under the cover of twilight, a feint meant to bait the defenders into panic. But Astryd had seen through it. She didn't panic.

Tonight, she would be the one to strike first.

No war cry was given. No horn blew. The silence became its own kind of sacred.

They moved like smoke through the valley. Hopps ranged ahead silent, precise eyes catching the faintest glint of steel or wrong movement in the trees. He cut a forward path with barely a gesture. Just a flick of his fingers, the twist of his boot in soft earth.

Astryd followed with Blu at her back, their forces moving in tight formation. Not a single footstep wasted. Not a single breath out of place. Every warrior here followed her not because they were ordered to. Because they believed.

The cliffs narrowed as they approached the pass. Astryd signaled the halt with two fingers. They dropped low, disappearing into the terrain.

Blu closed her eyes. *"He's here."*

Astryd didn't flinch. **"Let him watch. He won't like what he sees."**

She motioned again. Scouts flanked left and right. Within moments, three sharp beams of light lanced into the sky the signal.

Go.

Astryd didn't hesitate. **"Engage."**

They surged.

The strike landed like a thunderclap. Hopps was the first to clash steel, slicing clean through a shadow bound skirmisher's throat before he even drew breath to warn.

Astryd followed like a storm her power surged through the relic, feeding into the earth, setting the ground beneath them alight in lines of searing gold. The first wave of Malrec's men fell not with screams, but with disbelief. They had not expected her here. Not this fast. Not this strong.

She moved through their lines like flame catching dry grass. Her blade found joints in armor like it had memory. Her spells twisted through the battlefield like coiling serpents. She didn't just command. She consumed.

From the ridge, Blu dropped barriers between enemy groups, isolating them like prey caught in a trap. Her staff struck the ground and the runes along her robes flared, a wave of divine light shattering shadow magic on contact.

Behind them, the warriors rallied. Shields locked. Arrows flew with precision. Not one of them faltered.

An armored brute tried to flank Astryd, a wicked blade raised Hopps met him head-on. His knife was a whisper in the dark, buried between the ribs before the man could blink.

Astryd turned just long enough to see the silent thanks in his eyes. He didn't speak it. He didn't need to. He signed quickly: *You're not alone. Keep going.*

She did. She burned.

The clash lasted less than twenty minutes. That was all it took. The first strike wasn't just victory it was devastation.

They regrouped on the ridge, the battlefield behind them littered with ash, broken steel, and silence.

Astryd stood tall. Her chest heaved, her skin streaked with soot and sweat, but her grip on the relic never faltered. It glowed against her chest like a heart reborn.

Hopps approached, his hands signing slow, steady. They followed you. They believed. And they were right to.

Blu joined them, her voice low, her tone even. *"The strike worked. But this wasn't the war. This was the opening."*

Astryd didn't look away from the horizon. Somewhere, Malrec would be watching. He would feel this loss. He would lash out.

Good.

"Let him," she said. ***"We'll meet him at the gates of every city he dares approach. And this time..."***

She turned. The light in her eyes wasn't wild anymore. It was focused. Feral. Chosen.

"...we burn on our own terms."

Chapter fifty one: Bound by Fire

The battlefield still smouldered beneath their boots. Smoke clung to the air like a ghost that refused to leave, and the scent of blood, sweat, and scorched earth mingled with it, settling deep into the fabric of their clothes. Ash streaked the edges of their cloaks, dried blood hardened on armor that hadn't seen rest in hours, but no one in the command tent bowed their heads.

They had survived the first strike and more than that, they had claimed the upper hand. Not just over ground or enemy formations, but something bigger. Something more vital. They had taken control of the story being written here.

Astryd stood at the head of the makeshift war table, her gloves discarded, hands stained from fire and magic and battle. Her fingers were calloused and cracked, nails lined with soot and blood, but they were steady. The relic pulsed softly against her chest, its once-wild energy now calm. It didn't rage. It waited. Not asleep attentive. Obedient.

Around her, her lieutenants delivered updates in practiced cadence supply lines secure, scouts reporting enemy fallback, defensive runes recharged. Casualties were low. Morale was high. Momentum belonged to them.

But Astryd didn't speak right away. She listened.

Her eyes scanned the room. Every twitch, every breath, every flicker of uncertainty. And when the last voice went quiet, when the canvas walls stilled and even the wind beyond the tent hushed like it was leaning in to hear her speak only then did she lift her chin.

"They know we're not afraid of fire anymore," she said, voice low but unwavering.

Hopps stood at her side, arms folded. His stance looked relaxed, but every inch of him was alert. His gaze hadn't left her once not since the fighting stopped. And beneath the table, his fingers brushed hers for just a second. A reminder. A grounding point. His presence alone said what words never needed to.

You're not alone.

Blu stepped in from the outer ring, her robe lined in fading ward ink and stitched with prayers that had been cast and answered. Her hair was damp with sweat and spell light, and her hands still faintly glowed with divine residue. Her eyes locked onto Astryd's and held.

They had done more than survive this assault.

They had awakened something.

Astryd took a slow breath and stepped around the table, circling it like a flame looking for oxygen. *"Malrec believed we were fractured,"* she said. *"That I was unsure. He sent his shadows to test us."*

She paused, one hand resting on the edge of the table. Her knuckles whitened, but her voice stayed steady. *"But they broke first."*

A few of the gathered commanders exchanged glances. Someone whispered an oath of agreement. Another murmured a quiet "Damn right."

"I made a vow," Astryd continued. *"To fight not just with fury, but with purpose. And every one of you, you stepped into that fire with me. You chose to follow."*

Hopps signed beside her, quick and fierce. *We didn't follow because we had to. We followed because we saw what rises from ruin.*

Her eyes met his, and a flicker of emotion broke through the steel of her composure. Not weakness. Recognition. *"And we're not done."*

Outside, the camp stirred. Survivors of the strike some limping, some bandaged, most still streaked with blood gathered near the central stones. They didn't stand in ranks. They stood together.

Not because of orders, but because something had drawn them. A pull. A current in the air.

Astryd stepped out beneath the stars. The night was crisp, alive with energy. Every movement felt like a spark waiting to catch.

She didn't climb to a platform. She didn't rise above them.

She stood among them.

"What we did tonight was not survival," she said, eyes scanning every bloodstained face. **"*It was the beginning of reclamation.*"**

Blu moved to her right. Staff grounded. Cloak fluttering with unseen magic.

Hopps stood to her left. Blade still sheathed. His silence thundered with presence.

"We do not fight as scattered embers," Astryd continued. ***"We burn as one."***

She opened her hand. The relic responded. Heat not searing, but holy spread in a pulse through the ground beneath them. Sigils shimmered. Runes lit up. People gasped. Some dropped to one knee. Others whispered words of awe.

"*This is no longer about revenge. It's about what we protect. What we become. What we build from what they tried to take.*"

A hush fell. Then Blu spoke, voice sharp and clear. ***"She rose from the ashes of betrayal."***

And then quiet, guttural, beautiful Hopps spoke. Aloud. ***"And now she leads us to the pyre... not to die, but to forge a future."***

He hadn't spoken to anyone but Astryd in years. The air went still. Even the flames paused. Astryd turned toward him not surprised. Not shaken. But seen.

She reached out, her hand finding his, gripping tight. ***"We are bound,"*** she said, voice low but sure. ***"By fire. By choice. By blood."***

Then she turned and stepped down not above them, but into them. One hand in Hopps's, his grip solid as stone. The other clasped by Blu, who closed her fingers around Astryd's like sealing a promise in flesh and flame.

They stood like a trinity: shadow, flame, and light.

And the ember between them didn't fade.

It flared.

The camp didn't erupt into cheers.

It sang.

Low. Reverent. A hymn passed between warriors and mages and scouts and survivors. Not a song of war.

A song of rising.

A vow in the form of breath.

And somewhere deep in the dark, where the wind curled through trees and distant eyes watched from the edge of war...

The world shifted.

And it whispered her name.

Chapter fifty two: What We Carry Into Flame

Morning didn't break.

It rose slow and heavy, like steam rising from scorched earth, like breath held before a scream. The sky bled rust instead of gold, and the sun crept above the horizon with the weight of a blade being drawn. There was no softness in the dawn. No comfort. Just the slow, inevitable unfurling of another day in the shadow of war.

Within the camp, fires had already been rekindled. Not for warmth. Not even for food. These were ritual flames kept burning for memory, for clarity, for the sacred rhythm of preparation. Smoke curled into the sky like offerings, and the scent of ash clung to skin and armor alike.

Astryd stood in the centre of it all. Unmoving. Unshaken. The firelight caught on the edges of her cloak, casting flickers of shadow and ember across the hardened lines of her face. She looked carved from stone, kissed by flame. Her eyes swept across the camp—not commanding, not judging. Just watching. Absorbing. Bearing witness.

Around her, the world moved in a deliberate rhythm. Fighters sharpened their blades without speaking, their focus honed to a razor's edge. Mages marked protective sigils into bracers and helms, hands stained black with charcoal and old blood. Clerics whispered blessings into the wind, not begging for survival but promising remembrance.

There was no chaos here. Not anymore.

Only order. Discipline. And the kind of calm that came just before something ancient and terrifying was unleashed.

As Astryd moved through the camp, she saw them all. Her people. Her fighters. Her chosen. One soldier paused to string a braid of their daughter's hair into the leather grip of a blade. Another a weaver turned warrior threaded flame glass beads onto their friend's belt, murmuring, "*For luck.*" Their companion answered quietly, "*For fire.*"

Every act a ritual. Every silence a prayer.

And at the perimeter, where the warding stones met the edge of the trees, Hopps stood like a sentinel.

He hadn't moved for hours. Not out of fatigue he rarely showed that but because he didn't need to. His presence was steady, rooted. The kind of constant that made people believe in survival. His gaze swept the trees with clinical precision, and though his sword was sheathed, there was no question he could draw and kill in a breath.

When soldiers passed him, they offered respectful nods. Not for his title Hopps didn't care for ranks but because of what he'd done. Because he had spoken. Aloud. For her. The sound of his voice had silenced an army. And that kind of power, born of silence broken with purpose, commanded more than respect.

It commanded faith.

Blu moved with quieter gravity through the centre of the camp, her robes streaked with consecration dust and warding ink. Her staff did not glow, but the air shimmered faintly around her, like it remembered the miracles she had performed. She didn't bless blindly. She stopped, knelt, and looked each warrior in the eye. Her words were soft, but they struck deep.

"*You are not broken*," she told one young woman who trembled as she laced her boots. "*You are tempered.*"

To a healer who wept alone in the shadow of the supply tent, she murmured, "*Grief is not weakness. It is the cost.*"

And when she reached the centre of the camp, Blu knelt by the fire, dipped her hands in a shallow basin of water, and let the ashes smear her wrists. "*We carry them,*" she said, voice rising just enough for others to hear. "*And in doing so, we rise.*"

Astryd approached slowly.

She felt the weight of it as she moved not burden, exactly, but presence. The eyes on her. The legacy in her bones. The magic stirring beneath her skin, echoing through the relic resting against her chest. Her boots crunched softly on the gravel path, and when she stopped at the fire, the heat warmed her face but didn't touch the cold, quiet place inside her.

Blu looked up.

A moment later, Hopps appeared on her other side silent, of course, but not invisible. Astryd could always feel when he was near. It was like gravity realigned.

"I don't know if I'm still her," Astryd said. Her voice cracked on the words, low and rough with exhaustion. *"The girl from Valebright. The one who swore she'd never let anyone fall again."*

Blu rose to her feet, brushing ash from her palms. "*She's not gone,*" she said gently. "*She just doesn't fit in the same shape anymore.*"

Hopps lifted his hands and signed: **She became the fire she once feared.**

Astryd's throat tightened. "*I'm scared,*" she admitted. "*Not of the fight. Not of Malrec. I'm scared because I believe in us. Because the moment I believe, I know what I have to lose.*"

"**Then don't carry it alone,**" Blu said.

A beat passed. Then the relic flared. It pulsed once against her skin twice, three times. Not in alarm. In recognition.

Power surged through Astryd's limbs. Not fire this time, but memory. Her knees buckled as visions struck.

She saw her mother singing in a collapsing tower, blood running down her arms.

She saw Hopps lifting her from the mud during their first battle, eyes wide with something like awe.

She heard Blu's voice, whispering her name in the darkness when she thought she'd lost everything.

And she saw herself not a queen, not a warrior, not a symbol. Just a girl who had chosen to survive. When she came back to herself,

Astryd was kneeling, both hands pressed to the earth. The relic had dimmed to a warm ember against her chest.

She stood slowly. Steadily.

"I can't walk away," she said. *"And I won't."*

Blu stepped forward and placed her palm over Astryd's heart. *"Then carry us into the flame."*

Hopps joined her. He didn't sign this time. He spoke. Voice clear. Certain. A blade honed on silence.

"And we'll follow. Not because we must..." he said, "*...but because we choose to."*

Gasps echoed through the camp. People turned. Some fell to one knee not in submission, but in reverence. Because Hopps had spoken. Again. And that meant something.

Blu stepped up beside them, her voice lifting like a prayer.

"She rose from the ashes of betrayal," she said.

"And now she leads us to the pyre," Hopps finished. *"Not to die but to forge a future."*

Astryd turned slowly, facing her people. Her warriors. Her kin. And in a voice steady with fire, she said, *"We are bound. By flame. By choice. By blood."*

She stepped down from the firepit not above them, but among them.

Hopps took her hand. Grounded. Steady. Blu clasped her other. Sacred. Unshaken. And something ancient passed between them. A tether. A spark. The start of something greater than a war.

The night did not end in silence. It ended in song. Low and fierce, sung from tired throats and hopeful hearts. Not a war cry.

A promise.

And beyond the treeline, where shadows gathered and the dark waited with open jaws, the fire didn't die.

It deepened.

Because Astryd didn't just carry them into flame.

She was the flame they followed.

Chapter fifty three: The Fight

The storm didn't break it built. Slow. Relentless. The sky had turned black well before noon, and now it hung heavy and close, thick with the taste of iron and the weight of too much magic. Every breath stung. Every heartbeat carried pressure.

Astryd stood at the front line, boots planted firm in scorched grass, her sword at her hip and the relic pulsing steady at her chest. She said nothing. She didn't need to. Her presence alone rippled through the ranks like a command.

From the ridge opposite, the enemy emerged row upon row of shadow-bound warriors, their skin etched with jagged runes that glowed faintly with abyssal light. Among them walked constructs of bone and twisted steel, moving with unnatural grace. Spellcasters, warlocks, monsters pulled from dark realms she didn't yet know by name.

And at the centre, Malrec.

He moved through the ruin like he'd never left it. His violet robes were unmarred by dust, his expression untouched by fatigue. He didn't need to raise his voice. He simply raised a hand and the battlefield paused, like even the wind waited to hear him.

"This is your moment, Astryd," he said, calm and cruel. *"I gave you time. I gave you warnings. You think your little victory buys you freedom?"*

She stepped forward not far, just enough to be seen. Enough for her people to feel the earth shift with her movement. *"You lost your chance when you made this personal,"* she said.

Malrec tilted his head. *"I told you once this isn't about you."*

"No," she agreed. *"It's about all the people you stepped on to reach me. And I'm done letting you speak like their lives don't matter."*

His eyes narrowed. *"That relic has warped you."*

"It's refined me," she shot back. ***"The difference? I'm still standing on my own two feet. You've been hiding behind monsters since Valebright burned."***

That got to him. Just a flicker a twitch of the mouth, a tightening around the eyes. But it was there.

Blu stepped to Astryd's right, staff grounded in the soil, her robes trailing smoke. She didn't speak, but her presence crackled with divine tension, her magic thrumming just beneath the surface. She was ready.

Hopps stood silent to her left, fingers tapping once against his thigh. The signal was clear. He'd marked Malrec's position. He was waiting for the opening.

Astryd didn't blink. ***"You want the relic?"*** she said. ***"Come and take it."***

Malrec's smile vanished. He didn't waste breath on threats. His forces surged.

The first wave hit like a landslide soldiers snarling, spellcasters launching volleys of flame and necrotic energy. The field erupted in chaos. Astryd met it with fire of her own. The relic flared and her sword lit up with searing golden energy. She dove into the fray, carving a path through the corrupted ranks, her magic pouring through her body like molten light.

Hopps vanished from sight.

When he reappeared, it was behind enemy lines clean strikes dropping casters before their lips could finish their chants. One warlock fell without ever seeing the blade that ended him.

Blu moved through the ranks like a storm wrapped in silk graceful, radiant, devastating. Her staff burned with divine power as she healed the injured mid-battle and unleashed radiant blasts into advancing horrors. Wherever she went, the tide shifted in their favour.

On the far ridge, Malrec raised both arms. The sky cracked. A scream of power echoed across the battlefield.

Astryd turned her gaze toward him just in time to see the runes bloom across his skin deep and ancient and utterly wrong. This was no longer about pressure. This was annihilation.

Meteor Swarm. Disintegrate. Blight. All at once.

The battlefield lit up like a dying star.

Blu threw up a massive ward. Her voice echoed with divine fury as she anchored it into the earth. Astryd raised her hand and the relic responded drawing on her pain, her anger, her purpose and threw a shield of pure light over their forward line. Hopps darted through the chaos, cutting down enemy supports and dropping a Silence field to smother the enemy's second ritual attempt.

Then it happened. Malrec stepped forward and spoke a word that split the air in half. Astryd's heart stopped. She recognized it. So did Blu.

Power Word Kill.

But this time, Hopps wasn't fast enough. Not because he hesitated but because he was too far from her. The spell came for her like a viper in the dark.

The relic reacted first flaring, flaring again. Astryd's feet lifted from the ground, the magic pulsing against her skin as it fought to resist the pull of death.

Blu screamed a ward. Astryd fell to her knees.

The relic cracked down the centre just a fracture, just enough and the spell fizzled into sparks around her shoulders. Not undone. Not cancelled. But deflected. It had cost her something.

Her breath tore from her chest like a scream.

But she lived. And she rose. When she stood, everything changed. The battlefield slowed. Then burned.

She lifted the relic into the sky and cast Sunburst—not from fear, but from fury. The light ripped through the shadow ranks like divine wrath made visible. Screams rose. Fiends melted into ash. Constructs shattered.

Even Malrec shielded his eyes and took a step back.

Reinforcements arrived behind her. Rangers from the southern woods. Beast masters riding scaled direwolves. Archmages with skin inked in starlight. The line surged forward with her at the front.

Hopps reappeared beside her, bloodied but standing.

Blu's staff slammed into the ground, releasing a radiant shock wave that pushed the enemy ranks back another thirty paces.

Malrec's formation broke. And this time, he didn't leave a message. He retreated. Dragged back through a portal by his elite guard, snarling as the light seared his heels.

Astryd didn't chase him. Not yet.

She turned and raised her sword toward her people. Her voice cracked through the chaos like thunder.

"We hold this line," she called. "*Not just today. Always."*

The battlefield answered with roars and war chants.

Hopps signed beside her, a grin ghosting the edge of his mouth.

Next time, he signed*, you duck faster.*

Blu laughed, a ragged, beautiful sound. *"And next time, he dies."*

Astryd smiled, firelight catching in her eyes.

This wasn't the end.

But it was the moment they turned the tide.

Together, they had claimed the first true victory.

And they would burn the path forward one step at a time.

Chapter fifty four: The Ashes Left Behind

The smoke hadn't cleared.

It hung low over the ruined field like a heavy curtain, thick with ash and the iron tang of blood. The sky was bruised with clouds, the sun only a smear behind the haze. And beneath it all, the battlefield stretched silent and scorched, cratered from impact, littered with the remnants of war.

Astryd dropped to one knee not from injury, not from weakness but to feel the earth.

The heat still radiated through her boots. The ground was dry, charred, broken in places where magic and steel had torn through it like claws. Her fingers brushed the blackened soil, slow and steady, as if touching it would anchor her. The relic at her chest no longer hummed. It pulsed faintly, a low, steady rhythm that mimicked her heartbeat slower now. Calmer. Like it, too, was coming down from the edge.

Around her, the field was still. Not dead. Just… holding its breath.

Hopps stood a few feet away, eyes tracking her but giving her space. He understood this moment. She knew he did. He had felt the same pull when the dust settled and victory tasted like ash. There was triumph in what they'd done. But there was also loss. And fire always demanded a price.

Blu moved first.

She emerged from the line of wounded like a specter robes darkened with blood and soot, face streaked with sweat. Her braid had long since come undone, strands of silver and black clinging to her cheeks. But her movements were precise. Intentional. She stopped beside Astryd, lowering to one knee, and placed her hand gently atop hers.

"You held the line," Blu said softly. Her voice was steady, quiet, but it reached the marrow. *"Even when it tried to break you."*

Astryd didn't look up. Her jaw clenched. Her hands curled tighter into the earth. *"I felt it,"* she said. *"I felt what the relic could become. What I could become."*

Blu didn't flinch. *"And you stopped. You chose not to burn."*

Hopps moved closer, crouching across from her. He didn't say anything at first. Just reached out with one hand and signed, slow and deliberate: *You didn't burn. You chose.*

Astryd's gaze flicked up to meet his. For a moment, everything else the smoke, the cries, the noise of a camp trying to rebuild faded. Her breath hitched, and she gave the smallest nod.

Hopps added: *You still have us.*

She looked away, not to hide, but to gather herself. Around them, the wounded were being treated. Some groaned, others sat in stunned silence. Broken weapons lay strewn beside broken bodies. There was no cheering now. Only the sound of breath and movement and effort the sound of those who had survived trying to make sense of it.

"How many did we lose?" Astryd asked, her voice rasping with fatigue.

Blu didn't soften it. *"Sixteen. Two more may not make it through the night. We're doing all we can."*

Astryd's jaw tightened. Her spine straightened. *"Then we burn them with fire,"* she said. *"Not as casualties. As warriors. As protectors."*

Her voice carried, even without volume. The nearby soldiers paused. Listened. Heard.

Within the hour, the pyres were being built not haphazardly, but with care. Vine-wrapped logs, bound with cloth. Sigils drawn in chalk and blood. Each pyre marked with the names of the fallen, and those who had no names were given stones inscribed with runes of passage.

Astryd lit every single one.

She used no fanfare. No grand spell. Just fire drawn from the relic pure and clean, a spark of remembrance rather than destruction. Each body was sent into the flame by her hand. Not because she had to. Because she chose to.

They had followed her into battle. She would lead them home.

Hopps approached once the final pyre was lit. His clothes were streaked with ash, his brow marked with soot. He reached into his cloak and withdrew a small rune stone weathered, smooth, carved with old symbols of mourning. He knelt at the last pyre and placed it gently into the flame.

Then he signed: *For the ones who had no names.*

Astryd didn't speak. She simply nodded, throat too tight to respond.

Blu joined them, slipping between them to press her hands together. She bowed her head, murmuring a final prayer over the fire. The light from the pyres danced in her eyes.

"They walk ahead of us now," she said. *"May their names carry in the smoke, and their stories be remembered in the stars."*

As the flames roared into the dusk, the entire camp gathered not to weep, not to scream. But to witness. No music played. No speeches were given. Just the sound of fire and memory.

And when the sky finally darkened, the stars emerged clearer than they had in nights. Astryd tilted her head back, letting the silence wrap around her like a cloak.

The war was not over.

Malrec still lived. There would be more blood. More choices. More fire.

But for now, in the quiet between battles, they honoured what they carried. Who they carried. The names. The losses. The cost.

And for this one night, at least...

They stood together.

Alive.

Unbroken.

Burning.

Chapter fifty five: The Final Threat

The wind had not calmed not truly. It whispered now, cold and thin, dragging its icy fingers through the camp like a thief searching for what was left. Blood had dried into the cracks of the earth. Ash clung to tents and armor. The fires still burned, but not with celebration. Not with warmth.

They burned because they had to. Because this wasn't done.

Malrec had fled, yes. But not defeated. Not yet.

Astryd stood alone on the ridge, the same place they'd burned their dead the night before. She hadn't slept. Her armor still bore the stains of the last battle, and the relic at her chest pulsed with slow, relentless certainty. Not warning. Not rage. Something quieter. Steadier. It had become part of her now. There was no line between her soul and its power.

Below her, the camp moved like a wounded animal. Hopps coordinated the final preparations with silent speed his hands signing faster than most could track.

Mages gathered in tight circles, spell books open, fingers twitching with last-minute recalibrations. Warriors adjusted armor and spoke in hushed tones that never rose above the wind.

Blu found her on the ridge. She didn't speak at first. Just stood beside Astryd and stared out at the scarred horizon.

"They say the stars are misaligned," Blu said after a long silence. *"The moon is dimmer than it should be. The elements are restless."*

Astryd didn't turn. *"He's opening the gate."*

Blu nodded. *"And not just any gate. The final one. The one they buried beneath prophecy and blood."*

Astryd exhaled through her nose. *"Then it ends tonight."*

A scream rose in the distance high, layered, distorted. Not human. Not beast. Something *older*. Something that remembered the world before it had names. And then the sky cracked.

Not thunder. Not magic. Something *else*.

A jagged wound tore open above the western ridge, bleeding light and shadow in equal measure. Colour drained from the horizon as if the world itself recoiled from the rift. The air shifted, heavy with the scent of ozone and rot.

And from the rift stepped Malrec.

But this was no longer the man they had fought before. He had changed.

His body was barely his own anymore twisted by the magic he had dared to consume. Abyssal wings arched from his back, made of bone and void. His face shimmered with illusion, eyes burning with ancient, insatiable hunger. His voice when he spoke echoed as if layered through time.

"You were meant to open it," he said. *"Not stand in its way."*

Astryd stepped forward. Hopps flanked her left, silent as a blade unsheathed. Blu took the right, staff crackling with latent divinity.

"You talk like this was always your story," Astryd said. *"But I'm rewriting the ending."*

Malrec laughed, and it was a sound that made the earth groan. *"You think you have the strength to stop what I've become? You think you can hold back a tide of gods?"*

"I don't need gods," Astryd said, drawing the relic to the centre of her palm. It pulsed with heat alive, awake, *ready*. *"I have my people."*

Malrec raised his hands, and the rift widened. From it spilled nightmares creatures stitched from memory and shadow, born of worlds that no longer existed. Crawling, flying, screaming.

Blu whispered a prayer that shimmered across the battlefield like sunlight through stained glass.

Hopps vanished in a blink his blade already swinging through the first wave of creatures before they touched ground.

Astryd gripped the relic and felt its power lock into her bones like armor.

"No more running," she said. "***This is where we make our stand.***"

The sky bled fire.

The ground cracked.

And the final war began.

Chapter fifty six: The Victory

Dawn did not break.

It erupted.

Gold spilled across the battlefield like prophecy fulfilled, burning away the ash and shadow left in the wake of war. Smoke coiled around shattered weapons and bodies that no longer stirred. Fire still crackled in some of the fallen siege towers, and scorched earth steamed as the warmth of sunrise met blood still cooling on the soil.

But for the first time in too long, the silence that followed wasn't grief.

It was peace.

But only after fire.

Malrec's fortress had fallen but not quietly. The final battle had been a war song sung in screams and steel, in prayers shouted through bloodied lips, in magic so ancient it left the air buzzing long after the last spell had been cast. The earth had cracked beneath them. The sky had torn open above them. And through it all, they had endured.

Astryd had led the charge straight into the inferno. The relic pulsed like a second heart against her chest, its glow a halo of defiance and fury. Her steps were heavy with pain, but she never faltered. Every swing of her sword was a story: of survival, of vengeance, of devotion to the people behind her. The blade sang with divine heat, cleaving through Malrec's elite like flame through paper.

Each cut, each cry, was liberation. Not just from Malrec but from the ghosts that had haunted her since Valebright.

Blu had fought like a storm given form. She summoned holy fire from the heavens, her prayers no longer whispered, but wielded like weapons. Her voice, clear and unwavering, rang out with every spell. Her staff glowed like a star fallen to earth, and when she called Flame Strike down onto the abyssal horrors, even the demons flinched.

Wings of light unfurled from her back not symbolic, but real anointing her as more than a cleric. She had become justice.

And Hopps… Hopps was war in shadow.

He moved like smoke and struck like lightning. He weaved through Malrec's ranks with lethal precision, never stopping, never speaking, only acting. He was vengeance made flesh calm, calculated, relentless. He saw threats before they emerged and ended them before they could speak. One warlock tried to target Astryd. Hopps slit his throat from behind, then vanished before the body hit the ground.

They fought together. Seamless. Unyielding. Until they reached the altar. Malrec waited. Of course he did.

He stood atop the stones with darkness coiled around him like a crown, the stolen magic of a thousand souls seething beneath his skin. His voice crawled across the battlefield, laced with hunger and ruin.

"You refused your purpose," he snarled.

Astryd stepped into the circle, alone. The others held back not because she asked, but because they understood. This moment was hers. *"This ends with me,"* she said.

Malrec laughed, a bitter, splintered sound. He hurled his final curses **Disintegrate. Power Word Pain.** Magic meant to unmake.

The relic absorbed them like they were nothing.

Astryd didn't flinch. She moved. The first strike shattered his staff.

The second broke the shield around his heart.

The third, driven with all the strength she had left, buried her sword deep into his chest.

She leaned in, her voice low, intimate, final. *"You made me the flame. But I lit the fire."*

Then she pulled the blade free. Malrec burned not in anger, not in spectacle, but in the quiet fury of justice fulfilled. Light cracked across the sky. A sound like a dying star echoed through the earth.

When the smoke cleared, Astryd still stood shaking, bruised, bleeding but victorious. The relic pulsed once more beneath her ribs. Then, slowly, it dimmed.

Whole. Hers.

They had won.

Now, Astryd stood at the Center of what remained. Her cloak was torn, one sleeve ripped nearly off. Her hands were stained in blood that would never wash fully clean. Her hair tangled with soot and sweat, her breath still shallow but her eyes...

Her eyes were clear. *"It's done,"* she said, her voice breaking just enough to make it human.

The wind didn't answer. But her people did. One by one, the survivors emerged from smoke and rubble. Warriors. Mages. Riders. Rangers. All bloodied. Some broken. All breathing.

They came to her, not as soldiers to a general, but as kin returning home.

Blu reached her first. She limped forward, one gauntlet cracked, her robes burned at the hem. But her face shone, radiant with exhausted joy.

"He's gone," she said. *"Malrec is finally gone. The relic sealed him. The rift closed."*

Astryd turned to her, throat tight. *"And the others?"*

"We held the line," Blu said. *"Every flank. No losses after Hopps took down their last caster."*

She grinned through her cracked lips. *"He moved like a ghost. Scared the hell out of the enemy."*

Hopps appeared just then bloody, battered, barely holding his sword upright. But smiling.

Not the ghost-smile he wore in shadows. A real one.

He didn't say a word. Just crossed the distance between them and pulled Astryd into his arms. Held her like she was life itself.

And this time, she didn't pull away. She leaned in. Let herself feel it. Let herself believe they were still here. That she was still here. That it was over.

Victory didn't roar. It sang.

By midday, the battlefield had been cleared. Runes were carved for the dead etched into stone and bone, into earth and memory. Fires burned, not in fury, but in reverence. The air smelled of incense and ash, steel and mourning. And still hope.

On the highest ridge, Astryd stood. Her blade driven deep into the earth. The relic rested beside it dim, quiet, peaceful. Not as a weapon. As a promise.

She turned to them to Blu, to Hopps, to the others who had given everything.

"We don't go back," she said, her voice clear and strong. *"Not to the way things were."*

A murmur of agreement rose. *"No crowns. No tyrants. No shadows."* She looked across the hill. *"Just truth. Just light."*

Blu stepped forward, planting her staff into the earth beside the blade.

"Then let the first stone be set now," she said.

Hopps joined them. His shoulders relaxed for the first time in weeks. He looked at Astryd, signed one word: **Home.**

And then, with all the strength he had left, he spoke aloud for them all to hear: *"We survived fire. We survived blood. And now we rise."*

Astryd knelt. Pressed her palm to the scorched soil.

"Let this ground remember us," she whispered.

Above them, the sun broke through the last of the clouds. And in its warmth, something ancient and sacred sparked **Not an empire. A future.**

Chapter fifty seven: The Quiet Rebuilding

The fires had gone out.

Not the ones on the battlefield. Those had been quenched with blood, with magic, with sweat and will. No, these were the quiet fires the ones inside them. Burnt low, not extinguished. Resting. Waiting.

Astryd sat on the steps of what remained of the ridge's outer keep, a half-cracked column beside her and the relic resting, dormant, in her lap. The wind had shifted. Softer now. Like the land itself was beginning to breathe again. Her fingers curled loosely around the artifact. It no longer pulsed with desperate power. It simply existed. Like her.

She didn't look up when Hopps sat beside her. She didn't need to. The weight of his presence was familiar—steady, like the ground beneath her boots when the world started to tilt. He didn't speak. Didn't touch her. Just sat there in silence, shoulder to shoulder.

That was how she knew he understood.

She was still collecting herself. Still learning who she was after the fire.

"I don't know what comes next," she whispered, voice raw from too many orders and too many screams.

"You don't have to," he said softly. *"Just don't face it alone."*

She smiled faintly, more tired than amused. *"I'm not used to having a future to think about."*

Hopps reached out then, slow and deliberate. His fingers brushed hers over the relic. No pressure. Just contact. Shared warmth. Shared truth.

Blu appeared moments later. Her steps were slower, not from injury, but exhaustion that lived deep in the bones. She held a bundle of herbs and half-burned charms in one hand, her stave in the other. Her eyes found Astryd's, and something unspoken passed between them like a thread pulled taut.

"You feel it too," Blu said softly, lowering herself onto the step beside them. *"The shift. It's not just in the relic. It's in us."*

Astryd nodded. *"The land feels different. Like it's been... rewritten."*

"It has," Blu agreed, her voice low. *"By fire. By blood. By choice. And now,"* she added, looking to the horizon, *"we decide what we write next."*

There were no crowds. No applause. No ceremony. Just a handful of soldiers and survivors moving through the ruin with quiet reverence. Tending to the wounded. Repairing the broken. Drawing fresh warding runes in the dirt, not because they feared attack but because they remembered.

A dwarf knelt and cleaned the blade that had saved his brother. A mage, still bruised, passed a child a small glowing crystal. One woman sat by a fallen friend and whispered old songs from their childhood until the tears stopped falling.

The world hadn't healed.
But it had started to breathe again.

That evening, they lit a fire. Not for battle. Not for defense. But for warmth.

Astryd sat beside it, cloak loosened at the neck, boots scuffed and cracked. Hopps leaned beside her on one side. Blu took the other, cross-legged and quiet, her staff lying across her knees like a resting sentinel.

They passed food. Simple. Warm. Enough.
Someone played a flute with no rhythm.
Someone else hummed a lullaby that had no end.
The silence between them wasn't emptiness it was safety.

And then Blu leaned forward. Her voice was low, but it carried across the flames like prayer. *"Astryd. What you carry now... what the relic has become... it's no longer just a weapon. It's a symbol. Of everything you chose. Of who you are. Of who we are."*

Astryd looked down at the relic. No longer burning. No longer bound in pain or rage. Just warm. Steady.

She looked at Hopps.
At Blu.
At the fire.

"Then let it be carried by three," she said. **"Not one."**

Blu reached first. Her fingers brushed the edge, and the relic answered not with power, but with peace.

Hopps followed, hand resting on top of theirs. Not with demand. With devotion. And when Astryd placed her palm over both, the relic pulsed with quiet light. A steady glow.

Not fire.
Not command.
Unity.

They didn't speak after that.
They didn't need to.

The stars stretched above them, wide and infinite. The world was still cracked, but it was theirs now.

And for the first time since the fall of Valebright, Astryd let herself sleep.

Not as a weapon.
Not as a commander.
Not even as the bearer of the relic.

But as a woman held by those who saw her and stayed.

The rebuilding had begun.
Not with grand declarations.
But with three hands, resting on one relic.

And that was enough.

Chapter fifty eight: The Oath Beneath Ashes

The dawn broke not with fanfare, but with stillness.

A pale gold light spilled across the valley where so many had bled, where screams had once echoed. Now there was only breath soft, fragile, human. It was the kind of morning that could have gone unnoticed in another life. But today, it mattered.

Astryd woke to warmth. Not fire. Not power. Just the quiet weight of a blanket tucked around her shoulders, the soft hush of wind outside the tent, and the distant murmur of voices steady, calm, preparing for something she had not yet seen.

She blinked against the light. The relic at her chest felt cool for the first time in days, its heat replaced by something quieter. Not dead. Not dormant. Listening.

Outside, Blu stood barefoot in the ashes of the old battlefield. She moved with intention, her steps slow, deliberate, tracing circles in the earth with powdered stone and salt. Her voice, low and melodic, hummed a prayer in a language few remembered.

It was not for the gods.
It was for the fallen.
For those who had fought.
For those who had stayed.
For the pieces of themselves they'd lost to the flame.

When Astryd stepped out, the light touched her like an embrace gentle, golden, unthreatening. Hopps was already waiting. He didn't speak. He didn't need to. He just held out his hand, and for the first time, she took it without hesitation.

They walked together to the heart of the field where the final battle had been won. The ground here was scorched clean, blackened and hardened by magic and war. But now, a wide circle had been drawn. Precision in its shape. Reverence in its purpose. Within it, a mound of stones lay stacked each one carved or marked by those who had survived.

Blu stood at the edge, her robes drifting like smoke in the breeze. She raised her hands. The camp fell silent.

"This is not a burial," she said. *"This is a reckoning. Of who we were. Of what we lost. Of what we chose to become."*

One by one, the survivors stepped forward. Each placed a stone. Some bore names etched with trembling hands. Some carried symbols family crests, battle sigils, broken runes. Others were left blank, carrying the weight of grief too heavy to carve.

When it was Blu's turn, she knelt with quiet reverence. Her stone was smooth, worn, carved with the sigil of her first temple a place long lost to shadow. She pressed it into the earth with both hands and whispered a name no one else could hear. Her lips trembled, but her voice did not break.

Hopps approached next. His stone was small. Unmarked. But heavy with memory. He looked down at it for a long moment, his hand curled tight around it, knuckles white, before placing it among the others. No one asked what it meant. They didn't need to.

It was his story. And that was enough.

Astryd came last. She knelt slowly, the relic at her chest pulsing once, low and even. She took a flat piece of obsidian and dipped her finger into soot and ember. Carefully, deliberately, she scrawled a single word onto the stone's surface.

Valebright.

She pressed it into the centre of the circle.
Not to forget.
But to lay it down.
To say goodbye.
To begin again.

She rose. Her shoulders squared. Her voice, when it came, was steady.

"We are not what we've destroyed. We are what we've saved."

The wind picked up, catching the frayed edges of her cloak and the ends of Blu's braids. The ashes whispered. The valley listened.

"We were forged in fire. And now, we rise in its light."

Blu stepped forward, her voice soft, but no less fierce. *"This isn't a kingdom. This is a vow."*

Hopps moved beside her, his hand to his chest. Then breaking the silence he spoke aloud, only the second time since the war had ended. *"This is no longer about revenge,"* he said. *"This is about what we protect. What we become. What we build when the flames recede."*

The hush that followed was reverent. Sacred.

Then Blu's voice rose once more. A final blessing. A familiar rhythm. *"She rose from the ashes of betrayal."*

Hopps answered without hesitation. *"And now she leads us to the pyre—not to die... but to forge a future."*

Astryd turned to look at them. Her people. Her partners. Her fire.

And with the wind at her back and their hands in hers, she said the words that sealed the next step of their story: *"We are bound. By fire. By choice. By blood."*

She stepped down not above them, but among them.

One hand in Hopps's. One hand clasped by Blu. Together. And something ancient passed between them. Not power. Not command.

Trust.

The ember of something vast sparked in the space between them—and caught. The night didn't end in silence. It ended in song. A low, rising hymn that moved like breath through warrior's lips and cleric's voice. Not a war cry. **A promise.**

And as the stars wheeled above them, Astryd knew: The relic's power would no longer define her. **Their bond would.**

This was how a new era began. Not with a sword. Not with fire. But with an oath. **Beneath the ashes of all they had lost They built something that would never burn again.**

Chapter fifty nine : Where Magic Breathes

The ruins of the old sanctum stood like bones half-buried in the earth, weathered by time and war, touched now by the light of a dawn that felt... different.

This was no battlefield. No war council ground. No temple of gold and glory. This was the heart. And it had stopped beating long ago.

Blu stood at the edge of the cracked threshold, eyes closed, fingertips pressed to the scorched stone. The wind moved through her braids like it, too, remembered what had been lost here.

Astryd stood behind her, the relic cradled in her hands quiet now. Receptive. No longer just a source of fire, but resonance. It didn't hum or surge. **It listened. It felt.**

She could feel it, pulsing gently in sync with something far older than her heartbeat. As if it remembered the way this place used to breathe.

The ley lines beneath the sanctum had been severed during the last wave of Malrec's magic twisted, starved, nearly shattered. Their task wasn't to control them. It was to help them remember.
It was to *heal* them.

"Are you sure I'm ready for this?" Astryd asked, her voice lower than the morning wind.

Blu didn't open her eyes. *"You don't need to be sure,"* she said softly. *"You just need to be open."*

Hopps stood just beyond the archway, a silent sentinel. His eyes swept the treeline, the cliff edges, the sky but always returned to her. To Astryd. To the way her shoulders moved with every breath, like she still wasn't used to the weight being hers alone.

She had changed the world with fire. Now she would change it through *presence*.

Blu began the ritual with breath not words, just sound. She knelt at the center of the cracked floor and laid four stones around her, each etched with a different celestial sigil. Air. Earth. Water. Flame.

She pressed her palms to each in turn. The stones responded humming faintly, their glow warming like an old memory waking up.

"Astryd," she said, *"step into the centre. Barefoot. Nothing between you and what sleeps below."*

Astryd hesitated. Then she removed her boots and stepped forward, feet bare against the cracked stone. It was cool. Not lifeless. Just waiting. She moved to the middle of the circle, the crystal veins beneath her feet barely pulsing.

She knelt. The relic pulsed in her hands. And then she closed her eyes. She didn't speak. She *listened*.

At first there was nothing. Only the tension in her chest, the echo of breath and heartbeat and something else fear.

But then... something deeper.

A whisper in the stone. A tug in her spine. A lullaby in a language she had never learned, but had always known.

Not a voice. A remembering.

She reached out not with power, but with *presence*. And the earth *answered*.

It came slowly. Carefully. Like music with no melody just feeling. The ley lines stirred beneath her. Not in pain. In trust. They had *waited* for this. For her.

Light spilled from her fingertips, glowing soft and sure. The relic responded, not with dominance, but with *offering*. Threads of warmth spun from her palms, sliding into the cracked floor and finding the broken pieces of sigils, binding them back together.

Outside, Hopps watched in stillness. He had seen her tear down empires. He had watched her burn through the dark. But this — this quiet miracle this *mending* struck deeper than war ever could.

He wasn't witnessing power. He was witnessing peace.

Blu stepped back as the stones glowed brighter. Air. Earth. Water. Flame. Not aligned by control, but by harmony.

Astryd opened her eyes. And the sanctum *glowed*. From the centre, a column of light rose not sharp or burning, but braided like thread. Each strand carried something different: survival. Unity. Sacrifice. Love.

The light climbed skyward, weaving itself into the clouds, painting the grey with hues of copper and gold. A beacon not of dominance, but of ***promise.***

Astryd stood, slowly. Her body trembled. Not from magic. From *relief.*

"I heard them," she whispered. ***"The land. The magic. They're not afraid anymore."***

Blu came to her side. ***"Because neither are you."***

Hopps stepped forward, his footsteps quiet on stone. He didn't speak. He knelt beside her and placed one hand on the sigil now burned into the floor.

Astryd reached down and offered her hand.

He took it.

Blu joined them, her palm closing over both.

In the space where magic once meant war, they built something else.

Not a weapon.
Not a wall.
A *vow.*

This time, the world would be rebuilt not from conquest or command
but from **connection.**

Magic didn't demand fear anymore.
It breathed.

And it breathed with them.

Chapter sixty: The Flame That Remains

The sanctum stood whole once more.
Not as it had been not untouched or unmarred but rebuilt with hands that knew loss, and hearts that had chosen to love anyway.

Morning bathed the stones in gold. Wind threaded through the high arches, carrying the faint hum of restored ley lines. The magic that had once twisted in resistance now flowed in steady rhythm, a song of balance, of breath, of life.

Astryd stood at the centre of the sanctum, cloaked not in armor, but in a simple mantle of crimson and ash. The relic hung around her neck, pulsing quietly. It no longer demanded.
It responded.
Not power. Not prophecy. Presence.

Around her gathered the people she had saved, fought with, wept beside. Hopps. Blu. The warriors who survived. The mages who stayed. The villagers who had brought offerings wildflowers, river stones, handmade charms, and bread baked with trembling hands.

There was no throne.
No crown.
Only choice.

Blu stepped forward first, her cleric robes dusted with warding chalk, hands steady as she lifted a carved torch from the altar. *"This is not a coronation,"* she said. *"It is a declaration. A vow."*

She looked to Astryd, then to the people. *"This is what rises from fire. Not rule. But renewal."*

She lit the brazier in the centre of the sanctum. The flame caught soft and golden. Not wild. Not consuming. Inviting.

The crowd didn't cheer.
They *breathed*.
As if something inside them had been waiting for this moment to exhale.

Hopps stepped forward next. This time, he did not sign. He spoke. Clear. Sure.

"I never thought I would speak aloud again," he said. *"I thought silence was safer. Quieter. That words weren't worth the weight."*

He looked to Astryd, eyes steady, voice unwavering.

"But she taught me there is power in being heard. And you" his gaze swept the crowd *"you taught us all that surviving isn't enough. We have to live."*

The silence that followed wasn't empty. It was sacred.

Astryd stepped forward, taking her place beside the flame. The relic pulsed once warm, steady then stilled. She looked to Hopps, to Blu, to the others. She saw battle-scarred warriors standing beside healers. Children gripping parents' hands. Elders with tears they hadn't yet found language for.

"We do not rise from this with clean hands," she said. *"We carry what was burned. What was broken. What we could not save. But we carry it together."*

Her voice deepened. It didn't waver. It *anchored*.

"I will not rule over you. I will not rebuild an empire. I will walk with you. Shoulder to shoulder. As protector. As firekeeper. As one of many."

A soft murmur rippled through the gathered crowd. Relief. Recognition. Reverence.

Blu came to her side. Hopps did the same. Together, the three of them reached toward the brazier. They placed their hands over the flame not to claim it. To tend it.

The fire did not flare.
It did not roar.
It breathed.

From the arches of the sanctum, magic spilled like dawn through fog. A ripple of warmth and renewal passed over the land. Far below, in the villages nestled between rivers and ruins, crops stirred green and new. Wards pulsed with fresh light. Somewhere, a child laughed high and unafraid and others followed.

For the first time in years, the world didn't hold its breath.

It *sang*.

Astryd smiled. Not because the war was gone. But because the wounds no longer bled alone. Because healing had found root. Because they had remembered how to begin again.

They had not just survived.
They had changed.

From ash and agony, something new had taken root.

Not a kingdom.
Not a throne.
But a *future*.

Forged by fire.
Guarded by choice.
And held in the hands of those who refused to let the world burn without building something beautiful from its smoke.

The story did not end in flame.
It *began* there.

And beyond the sanctum, in the breath between one moment and the next, the flame remained.

The end

Epilogue: Ashes Remembered

The sanctum stood in silence.

No longer fractured. No longer haunted. It stood rebuilt by hand, by magic, by will. Etched into its foundation were names, not of rulers or saints, but of the fallen, the brave, the redeemed. This was not a monument to war. It was a promise.

Astryd stepped through the archway first. Not in armor. Not with the relic blazing at her chest. But in quiet robes, her shoulders unbowed. Her hair was streaked with silver from the magic she'd carried, her gaze steadier than it had ever been. The light in her eyes was not fire.

It was peace.

Hopps waited for her at the base of the sanctum steps, hands tucked behind his back. His voice had become steady since the battle. Used sparingly, yes. But when it came, it struck true. He smiled as she approached, and this time, it wasn't a warrior's smile. It was *his*.

"You're late," he said.

Astryd rolled her eyes, and for a moment, they were just people. Not legends. Not weapons. Not myth.

Blu stood at the altar within the sanctum, her hands glowing faintly as she laid the last of the crystals into the new leyline core. The chamber pulsed once. Then again. A heartbeat of magic slow and steady. *"It's ready,"* she said. *"The land is listening."*

Astryd turned to them both. *"Then let's speak."*

Together, they lit the final flame. A small brazier at the sanctum's heart caught with silver fire. No roar. No burst. Just warmth. Invitation.

The doors were opened to the realm not to kingdoms or crowns, but to all who had endured. All who had dared to rise.

From the hills came farmers with cracked hands and sharp eyes. From the woods, druids with leaf-crowned staffs. From ruined cities, smiths and scribes. The survivors. The seekers. They came not for power. But for purpose.

And at the heart of it all, three stood bound by blood, by vow, by choice. Not gods. But guardians.

The relic had changed. No longer a weapon, but a vessel of remembrance kept not on Astryd's chest, but in the sanctum core. Fed by many. Feared by none.

In time, songs were sung of the fire-born queen, the silent sword, and the cleric who healed not just wounds but the world.

But they were just people.
People who chose to stay.
To protect.
To rebuild.

And in the ashes of all that had been lost, something beautiful had begun.

A future.
One worth everything they had burned to reach.

THE END

Coming Soon: Sanctum of Flame

The war was over.
The ashes had settled.
But the fire inside us?
It never died.

A year has passed since the world cracked beneath our feet, since the relic chose me and we chose each other.
Now, new shadows stir beyond the horizon.
New voices call. Old wounds ache.
And new allies emerge fierce hearts bound by magic and loyalty.

The ashes have settled. The fire has forged a new path.
But the world beyond the sanctum is darker, deeper and the flame you thought you knew is only just waking.

New faces will enter the circle wild, fierce, unpredictable.
Old bonds will be tested.
Magic will twist and turn, burning everything you thought was certain.

The sanctum waits.
The flame flickers.
And I know this is just the beginning.

Astryd's fight is far from over.
This time, it's not just about survival.
It's about what you choose to protect…
And what you're willing to burn to build it.

Prepare yourself.
Because this time, the storm is not just mine to wield.

Let it burn.

BONUS CHAPTER: THE BEGINNING OF SANCTUM OF FLAME

Chapter One: Where Peace Starts to Crack

The wind still carried the scent of ash, even after a year.

Not the choking smoke of battle or the acrid bite of a city aflame, but a softer memory embers glowing quietly beneath cold earth. It clung to the stone of the sanctum and drifted on the edges of Astryd's breath whenever she let herself pause long enough to notice.

She stood on the eastern ridge, her crimson cloak snapping in the gentle morning breeze. Behind her, the sanctum tower gleamed, repaired and proud a monument and a promise both. Below, the land stretched lush and green where scorched earth had once screamed, fields of crops rising where blood had soaked deep. People rebuilding. Healing.

They called it peace.

But peace was not silence.

It was a different kind of armor quiet, heavy, and forever scarred.

"You're brooding again," came a voice behind her smooth, mocking, unapologetic.

Astryd turned.

Phil McCrakin strutted up like he owned the sky, his feathers gleaming in the sun, grin wide enough to steal it. An Aarakocra bard, professional teaser, and the most infuriating pain-in-the-ass anyone could love.

"Phil," she said flatly, *"it's not brooding. It's leadership."*

"Ah, the stern jawline of command. Is that scowl an upgrade or standard issue?"

"Do you ever enter a conversation normally?"

"Only when I'm trying to get laid."

"Phil—"

"Which, let's be honest, is basically always."

She sighed a long, dramatic sigh that said *I love you, but I'm too tired for this right now.*

Phil flopped his lute over his shoulder like a badge of honour. **"Come on, General Inferno. Admit it you missed me."**

Before she could remind him that **'missed'** was a strong word for **'annoy the hell out of,'** a softer voice cut through the morning.

"Astryd?"

Blaise stepped forward, sunlight wrapped in ember-red hair. A Fire Genasi druid and calm in any storm. Flames danced softly on his fingertips, warm but never scorching.

"I brought the wardstone samples you requested," he said, handing her a satchel. **"And some of Charm's salve. You've been pushing yourself too hard."**

She accepted the pouch, fingers brushing his longer than she intended. **"Thank you."**

Phil immediately doubled over, clutching his chest as if she'd just crushed his soul. **"Gods, can we please hold off on the lingering touches before breakfast?"**

Blaise's eyes sparkled with quiet amusement. **"Would you like a lingering touch, Phil?"**

His grin snapped back. **"Darling, I thought you'd never ask."**

Astryd didn't laugh, but the faintest twitch of her lips eased the weight she hadn't realized she'd been carrying.

They'd arrived three days ago Blaise and Phil envoys from the outer isles, disruptors of peace, a perfect balance between steady warmth and unpredictable chaos.

Behind them, the sanctum stirred.

Blu's voice drifted from the east tower, steady and calm as ever. Hopps moved like a shadow, training scouts in the courtyard. Deep within the sanctum's heart, the relic pulsed a new rhythm, urgent and raw a warning.

Something was coming.

Blaise stepped closer, fingers brushing Astryd's arm, sparking something she didn't want to admit she needed. *"You feel it too, don't you?"*

She did.

Phil's grin faded, his eyes sharpening with rare seriousness. *"The earth's restless. The winds are off. Something's waking."*

Astryd's gaze drifted north, to the jagged mountains on the horizon silent watchers of all that was lost and what was yet to come.

"Something's waking," she whispered. *"And we need to be ready."*

Phil flipped a dagger lazily, eyes alight with mischief. *"Looks like peace was just foreplay."*

She rolled her eyes. *"Do you have any setting other than inappropriate?"*

His grin widened. *"Would you like to find out?"*

Blaise snorted quietly. *"Phil."*

"What? I'm helping."

Phil smirked, nudging Blaise. *"Honestly, Blaise, the way you say 'let them come'... gods, you're downright sexy when you're ready to burn."* Blaise elbowed him.
Hard.

Astryd glared. *"If either of you say one more thing about me 'burning' or 'letting it go up in flames,' I swear "*

Phil spread his hands wide, innocent as a kid caught stealing cookies. *"Hey, I'm just here to light the fire."*

She exhaled, shoulders shaking. Damn him and his ridiculous charm.

The flame inside her hadn't died.

It was just waiting.

Phil leaned closer to Blaise, voice dropping to a conspiratorial whisper. *"If the world burns down, does that mean I finally get to see you naked in more than just battle scars?"*

Astryd blinked.

Blaise nearly choked on his breath.

Phil threw up his hands, grinning like a damned fool. *"What? I'm helping with morale!"*

Astryd glared so hard it might've cracked the air.

Phil winked.

Blaise sighed, shaking his head with a fond smile.

Astryd shook her head and smiled back.

Because despite the chaos, the teasing, the tension crackling like static between them this was family.

Wild, fierce, messy, unstoppable.

As the sun climbed, Phil plucked his lute and launched into a ridiculous, off-key ditty about fire, fate, and bad decisions, much to Blaise's feigned exasperation.

"You know, if you weren't so distracting, I might actually focus," Blaise said, folding his arms with a smile.

"Distracting? Me? Never!" Phil sang, grinning as he strummed with theatrical flair.

Astryd shook her head, laughing despite herself.

"Alright," she said, voice steadying with purpose, *"the relic's pulse is speeding. Blu said the wards are holding but barely. We're on the edge."*

Phil's smile slipped. *"Edge of what?"*

"War," Blaise answered quietly.

"And not the kind that comes with fanfare," Astryd said. *"The kind that creeps. Burns from inside."*

She felt the relic warm against her chest, alive watching, waiting.

Phil's grin turned serious, the edge of his usual teasing replaced with something sharp. *"Then we fight fire with fire."*

Blaise nodded, hands glowing as he gathered stray motes of flame from the air. *"And with earth, water, and air. All of us, together."*

Astryd drew a deep breath, the weight of the moment settling over her like a cloak.

"Let them come," she repeated. *"**We're ready.**"*

The wind shifted, carrying the scent of burning wood and something darker. Ancient. Waiting.

In that moment, she knew the fight was only just beginning.

Just as the last ember of dawn faded, a tremor ran through the ground beneath their feet sharp, unnatural, like the earth itself was tearing open a wound.

From the shadows beyond the sanctum, something ancient stirred.

And this time, it wasn't coming to negotiate.

The fire they thought they knew was about to consume everything.

END OF CHAPTER ONE

Author's Note

Astryd

Astryd's journey was never about perfection.
It was about power reclaimed through ruin.
About rage turned into clarity. About a woman rising from ash not to be saved, but to become the storm no one saw coming. She didn't heal because the world made it easy.
She endured because something inside her refused to break without meaning.
Because love deep, dark, chosen love dared to hold her when she forgot how to hold herself.

This is for the ones who have been cracked wide open.
For the ones rebuilding magic in bones that still ache.
For the ones who have carried too much, wanted too fiercely, burned too brightly and survived anyway.

For Hopps

Hopps's story was not loud.
It was not made of grand speeches or sharpened crowns.
It was made of presence. Of silence filled with meaning.
Of loyalty that never wavered not when the fire raged,
not when the world broke, not when *she* did.

He did not need to be the loudest in the room to be her match.
He stood at her side when no one else could.
Not to tame her, but to trust her.
Not to rescue, but to recognize.
Not to lead, but to walk beside her in the dark
with a hand held out and a blade ready.

This is for the ones who love without demanding.
Who listen louder than they speak.
Who protect not with noise, but with knowing.

Hopps taught us that devotion is not silence.
It's sovereignty, *shared*.

He didn't have to raise his voice to change the world.
He only had to say:
"I'm still here."
And *mean* it.

For Blu

Blu's magic was never about dominance.
It was about stillness in the storm.
About knowing when to hold the line
and when to hold the person.

She didn't come with fire. She came with roots.
With memory. With grace.

And in a world that burned, she offered the one thing even power couldn't guarantee: **Sanctuary.**

Blu didn't need to fight to be fierce.
She didn't need to shout to be heard.
Her strength was ancient
woven into the way she saw through
lies,   through pain, through pride
and loved anyway.

This is for the ones who carry healing in their bones.
Who never look away.
Who sit beside the broken without needing to fix them.

Blu reminded us that faith is not blind.
It's *chosen*.
That love is not always loud.
Sometimes, it's unshakable presence in a world that trembles.

She never left.
And in the end, her staying saved them all.

Acknowledgments

To Toni the heart of Blu.
Thank you for being my anchor when I couldn't breathe.
For picking up the pieces when I was too tired to hold them myself.
Your strength, your love, and your presence are woven through every line of this book.
This world exists because you never let me give up on it
or on myself.

To Sofie the heart of Hopps.
Thank you for giving me the spark that started it all.
What began as a joke during a D&D session
two characters sneaking off to the tents,
one warrior catching feelings while pretending not to
turned into a story that consumed us both.
We built this world together,
one look, one smirk, one stolen moment at a time.
You helped bring Astryd to life,
and I'll never stop being grateful.

To those who have been broken open and still dared to hope,
who chose to rise instead of retreat:
this story was written for you.

To the tabletop storytellers.
The dice goblins.
The late-night note app confession writers.
Never underestimate the power of tension across a D20.

And finally
to anyone who's ever been told they were too much:
Burn brighter.
Speak louder.
Take up your space.

This isn't the end.
It's the beginning of whatever you decide to build next.

With heat, love, and reverence,
Nesta Willard

To the Readers

You came here for bunnies and battle. You stayed for the tension
the kind that coils between spell casting and eye contact,
between a smirk and a threat, between a bard who talks too much
and a sorcerer who swore she wouldn't care.

You watched them circle, clash, flirt, and
fall.   You stayed through the magical misfires,
the one-bed-only nights, the curses that looked too much like desire,
and the moments when neither of them knew whether to kiss or kill.

And then Blu entered with the kind of stillness that breaks storms
and a spine forged of faith and quiet fury.

You saw her. The one who heals without asking for thanks.
The one who holds the broken pieces and dares to call it sacred.

You watched her anchor the flame, steady the chaos,
and remind them both that love isn't soft it's steel wrapped in grace.

Thank you
for letting these three ruin and rebuild each other in front of you.
For leaning into the fire. For turning the page even when it burned.
For understanding that sometimes, love looks like chaos wrapped
in consent, obsession laced with magic,
and surrender offered not in weakness but in power.

Not just between two, but three souls bound in fire-forged trust.

And to every writer who started with a dice roll
and ended up with a scene too filthy to say out loud at the table

You know exactly what this is.

You've felt the tension across the table. You've written the smut in
your notes app. You've looked at a bard and thought, ***oh no.***

So here's to you. Roll for inspiration. Then run with it.
Let it ruin your outline. Let it break your world in the best way.
Let the story take you somewhere you didn't plan
but never want to leave. With wild magic and wicked thanks,
Nesta Willard

THANK YOU

Thank you for walking through the fire with us.
For bearing the heat when it burned your skin raw,
and still standing fierce and unbroken.
For feeling every crack, every scorch, every wound,
and turning them into the fierce light that refuses to fade.

This book has been a whirlwind
a wild storm of pain and power, rage and redemption,
love laced with scars and strength forged in flames.
You've been with us through every blazing heartbreak and every ferocious victory,
and that fire inside you? It's just waking up.

Because the ashes have settled,
but the storm is far from over.
The next chapter waits heavier, hotter, and more relentless.
New faces, new battles, new fires to fight.

Are you ready to dive back into the blaze?
To rise again wilder, fiercer, untamed?

The flame you thought you knew is only the beginning.
Let it consume you.
Let it remake you.
And together, we'll burn brighter than ever.

www.ingramcontent.com/pod-product-compliance
Lightning Source LLC
Chambersburg PA
CBHW071659160426
43195CB00012B/1522